sensing God

This book is dedicated to my husband Alan,

who encouraged me to start writing,

but who did not live to see the completion of this book.

I hope that he would be proud.

sensing God

ideas and resources for creative worship

stella bristow

British Library Cataloguing in Publication data

A catalogue record for this book is available from the British Library

ISBN 1-85852-319-2 and 978-1-85852-319-4

First published by Inspire
4 John Wesley Road
Werrington
Peterborough PE4 6ZP

Printed and bound in Great Britain by APG

Acknowledgements

There are many people I wish to thank, but there is not space to name them all. However, there are some people to whom special thanks are due and must be recorded.

My children, Stephen, Alison and Debbie, and my daughter-in-law Helen, who never seemed to doubt my ability and were a constant source of encouragement. Jack, Rachel and Emily, my lovely grandchildren, for their unconditional love.

Mark Howard, not only for his stunning photography and layout but also for his helpful suggestions and enthusiasm.

Katharine Cheney, who patiently and with great humour worked on the initial editing and made helpful suggestions.

Natalie Watson at Inspire, for her encouragement and support.

Joan Sidaway, who, as well as being a good friend, gave invaluable help on aromatherapy.

Margaret and Colin Smith, for the use of their cottage in Devon, and Brian and Wendy Hartley, for the use of their home when I needed some space to write. Also, Mollie Locke and Pauline Squire, for ringing and writing regularly with words of encouragement.

Rachel Newton, Joyce and Brian Hoare, Eric and Pat Locke, Brian and Marion Fitzpatrick, Jill Fuller, Jill Greet, Kathryn Schofield and Margaret Sawyer, who all made helpful and encouraging comments on the early drafts.

My friends at Charlbury Methodist Church, for allowing me to try things out on them and the use of the church hall for photography.

Ann Leck, for all the encouragement, practical help, wise words and laughter we have shared together.

Rosemary Wass, without whose love and encouragement I doubt I would ever have finished this book. For all the time given to reading through drafts, for ideas at various points – not least the suggestion that this book might take shape as a recipe book – but, above all, for being there when I needed sisterly support and encouragement. Also to Howard Wass, for not only allowing me to disrupt the workings of a busy household with my frequent visits but also the stimulating discussions on theology that helped spark some of the creative process.

The Women's Network of the Methodist Church – my thanks to you all.

In the beginning was the Imagination
and the Imagination was with God,
and the Imagination was God;
and we beheld the glory of God's imagination
and God's imagination was the light of the world.

John 1 (adapted)

Contents

sensing God **introduction**

‘Everything in the mind has its origin in the senses.’

– St. Thomas Aquinas, ‘Summa Theologica’

sensing God introduction

Food for the soul

How many times have you received hospitality from friends and a particularly tasty dish on the menu has prompted you to ask for the recipe?

People have often asked me if I have any notes available on how to put together the various displays, meditations, music and symbolic activities that I use in services of worship, quiet days and retreats. In other words, 'Please could we have the recipe?'

This book is intended, not to give recipes exactly, but to suggest some good ingredients from which nourishing dishes can be produced. It's important to create your own style of menu to suit diverse palates. There is no right or wrong way. Have a go and see what works. Sometimes the most exciting dishes are created by accident! Remember, though, creative worship isn't an easy option. It takes more time, energy, foresight and practice than you might think and it must be done well.

The list of ingredients

Each chapter contains:

- **the retelling of a biblical story**
- **a personal story**
- **exercises**
- **worship material**
- **suggestions for music**
- **visual displays**
- **symbolic and tactile activities**
- **meditations and reflections.**

How you use these varied ingredients is up to you. Dip in or out, mix and dish them up in a different order. Allow your own imagination and prayerful thought to add an extra dimension to the way in which you use the material. I hope these ideas will provide you with resources to create stimulating, helpful worship and displays.

The first five chapters each focus on one of the senses – sight, hearing, taste, smell and touch. Two further chapters are offered – 'Seasoning', which has smaller items of worship to provide the herbs and spices to add to your worship recipes, and 'Extra portions', which are larger worship resources that stand on their own.

The larder

We are our own storecupboard of resources. We carry within us the ability to dream and imagine and to respond, through our senses, to that divine spark deep inside.

Banners and wallhangings

When we look at the same things week after week in church, after a while they can lose their impact. Sometimes it aids worship to have something different on which to focus. Many churches use attractive and colourful banners or wallhangings, created either for permanent display or to provide a visual aid for a specific season or point in the Church's year.

It is important that seasonal ones are removed. Don't leave Easter banners hanging until Christmas! If you make new banners or wallhangings, be sure beforehand that you know you have space in which to display them.

Worship centres

You may wish to create a worship display occasionally instead of a flower arrangement, using materials relating to the theme of the service. Creating displays requires a squirrel mentality – an eye for seeing potential in a piece of wood or a stone and in other people's rubbish as well as your own! As you gather items together, you may need to dedicate some storage space to your collection.

For many of the displays described here, I have suggested the use of fabric as a basis. This will be your most expensive item, but don't skimp on it. If you intend to create floor or table displays, be prepared to buy between 8 and 10 metres of specific colours. You can always fold or bunch any surplus and drape it so that it doesn't look too organized, but you can't make it go further if you don't have enough. You don't want it looking like a tablecloth!

Start with basic colours that reflect creation, so have a variety of browns, blues and greens. These will give you a background or base for most displays. You can then add other colours to represent seasonal variations: reds and yellows for Pentecost, gold and silver for Advent and the Christmas season, materials such as tweeds and hessian for Lent. There is a wonderful variety of cloth available today – shiny, sparkly and plain, with lovely textures and weights. Indian sari shops and market stalls usually have exciting and inexpensive fabrics.

A display is intended to create an *impression* of something, not a true visual representation of it. Let people use their imaginations. If someone asks, 'What does it represent?' ask what *they* see in it. As worship progresses, links will be made.

The use of subtle lighting and candles can help displays to 'live', but be aware of safety precautions. When using tealights, it is safer to use a simple gas lighter than matches or attempt to light them from each other.

All sorts of things can be used in displays: greenery, plants, shells, stones, sand, earth, figures, pots, candles and other visual aids. If you can't find fresh greenery and plants, don't discount fake ones. Some excellent artificial plants can be obtained from garden centres and, mixed with a little real foliage, can appear very realistic.

Where you have plenty of space, make your displays a good size so that people can see them.

There is nothing more frustrating than being a few rows back in a room or behind a church pillar and unable to distinguish the visuals. Ideally, worship in the round, with the display in the centre on a large table or the floor. Where this is not possible, use your imagination. You could have several 'stations' or build a display and invite people to come forward and view. I have never yet been to a church where this has been impossible. Try some of the displays suggested here and, even better, experiment with your own.

Small can be beautiful, too. Some lovely little worship centres can be made for a small-scale group meeting or congregation or for your own quiet corner at home. Use a low-level coffee table with material and, perhaps, flowers, candle or tealights or an appropriate artefact, but keep it simple.

A water theme display which could be used as part of the 'Waves of Change' worship centre, or adapted to reflect any of the biblical sea stories.

Music

Music can enhance worship enormously and you needn't stick to 'religious' music. There are some very evocative pieces written as themes to films, such as *Jurassic Park, Schindler's List, Saving Private Ryan, Raiders of the Lost Ark, Pride and Prejudice* and *Narnia.* Familiar classical favourites give endless possibilities. Remember, though, that choosing music to accompany prayers or readings or to provide the backdrop to a period of reflection takes a great deal of time, sometimes much longer than choosing hymns, so don't rush it.

Some points to consider:
- use background music for prayers or for topping and tailing readings
- ensure that the timing is absolutely right
- fit the words around the music
- make sure that the style of music chosen is appropriate
- when accompanying words, don't choose choral music to play in the background
- people with hearing difficulties may find background music a distraction
- ensure that playing equipment is in good order
- do not turn music off abruptly – fade the tape or CD in or out
- put all the music needed on to one tape or CD to avoid having to change them during the service
- provide operators of any sound system with explicit written instructions
- ensure that everyone is aware of the atmosphere you wish to create
- keep everything moving as smoothly as possible
- vary things from time to time.

New technology

The various kinds of projection equipment now available are wonderful tools that can be used in worship, but they need to be used wisely. Appropriate images can really enhance prayers and meditations. Words of hymns, especially new ones, can be well displayed. This may be helpful to those who are hard of hearing, but don't forget the needs of those whose eyesight does not enable them to read from a screen and who will still need printed handouts. Beware the temptation to put the entire service on a screen. To display the words of the celebrant in a Communion service can cause everyone to be so busy watching the screen that they fail to see the drama of the bread and wine being raised before them.

Coming to our senses

A medieval philosopher once said that everything in the mind has its origin in the senses. The most significant events of our lives are experienced through one or more of our senses. Yet, when it comes to worship, so often we seem to be locked into styles that seldom encourage or enable us to experience God in this way.

All our senses are involved in the enjoyment of food: sight and smell whetting our appetite, touch and taste enabling us to savour it and even hearing contributing to the experience. In Dickens' *A Christmas Carol,* Tiny Tim was borne out into the washhouse that he might hear the pudding singing in the copper.

This style of display would be useful for a retreat where it can be a focus for reflection on a number of different themes.

We learn through sight, hearing, touch, taste and smell. In each of us, one of these senses is dominant. Some receive information and understanding primarily through visual stimuli, others through touch. If we learn to use *all* our senses when engaging or reflecting on any activity, it will help to aid memory, because then we will be able to access information or signs through each sense.

'Words, words, words. I'm so sick of words,' sings Eliza Doolittle in the musical *My Fair Lady*. We bombard people with words in church, sometimes without giving enough time for them to filter through and lodge in their minds. Worship is often designed to appeal primarily to the intellect, rather than to the senses.

I believe that one of the tasks of the Church today is to enable people to recognize the God that is already active in their lives. We all have 'God' experiences, but many people don't recognize them for what they are and we don't always offer worship that allows for this to happen. For many, a church is an alien environment, where the worship offered is not relevant to their lives and does not take account of their feelings, but speaks in archaic language, with outdated images and, at times, in uncomfortable surroundings. Those who do venture over the threshold don't always feel at home. Many see nothing of relevance to them in what churches offer, yet are desperate to find a deeper meaning to their lives and search in all sorts of other places to explore their own spirituality. We need rituals and symbolic acts in worship, not only for births, marriages and deaths, but also for other things that people struggle with, such as divorce, separation, sexuality, redundancy, unemployment and ill health.

A section of table setting designed to accompany the 'Remember Me' worship material.

This simple display could be used throughout Lent, with additions for each weak. On Easter Sunday, the fabric cold be changed and the crown decorated to reflect the resurrection.

Jesus said, 'The kingdom of heaven is like a treasure hidden in a field.' Gerard Hughes in his book *God of Surprises* (Darton, Longman & Todd, 1996) suggests that *we* are the field and the treasure already lies hidden in us, waiting to be explored. The treasure is God.

Archbishop Desmond Tutu says that we are all 'God carriers'. We, who are made in the image of the divine, have a spark of the divine within us, there to be discovered and to be recognized in others, too. We are all spiritual beings and all contain that spark of the divine, but it needs nourishing with a varied diet. So ...

- be brave in experimenting
- be honest in reflection
- be willing to help others taste new experiences

and, above all, enjoy exploring God through your senses.

This was designed to be used with the 'Christmas Voices' worship, but it could be adapted for use during Advent, Christmas and Epiphany.

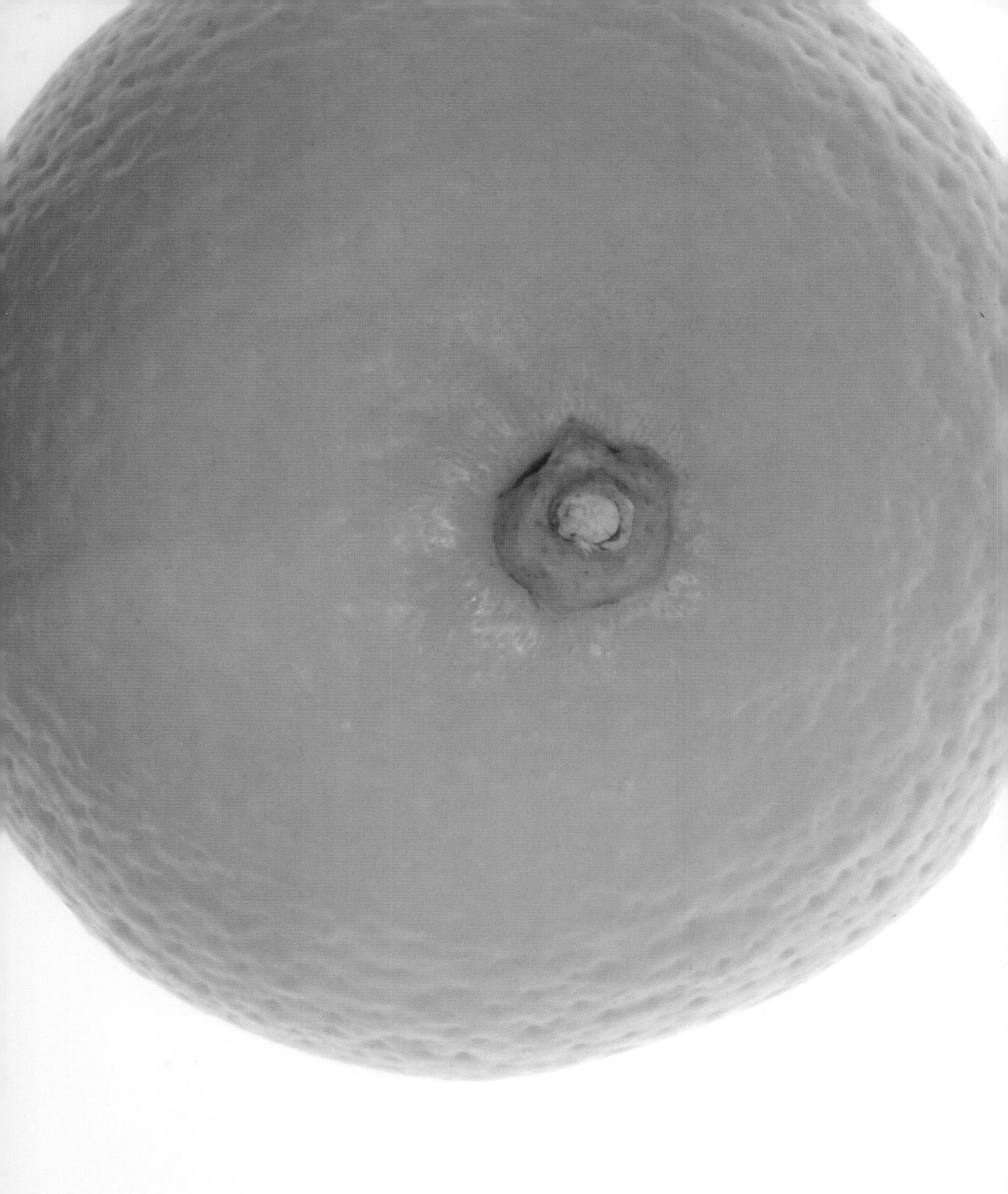

chapter one **fragrant memories**

**'There is a fragrance about you:
the sound of your name recalls it.'**

– Song of Songs 1.3 (GNB)

chapter one
fragrant memories

Our sense of smell is 10,000 times more sensitive than our sense of taste and we are able to distinguish thousands of different smells. The receptors that sense smells occupy an area about 2 cm square in the roof of the nasal cavity. When these receptors are stimulated by a smell, they transmit impulses to the part of the brain that deals with emotions. That is why response to smell is very personal. It is the most baffling and evocative of our senses, pressing buttons nothing else can, and often catches us by surprise. It is quite difficult to predict the effect a particular smell may have on a person as it depends on the emotion it triggers – even the loveliest scent or aroma can produce a negative effect if we experienced it when we were ill or very sad. Smells are strongly linked to memory and leave long-lasting impressions.

For a long time after my husband Alan's death, even though his clothes and personal items had been removed, I could smell his aftershave. Just now and then, when I opened a wardrobe door or the bathroom cabinet or moved a piece of furniture, I would briefly catch a hint of it. Not surprising perhaps, as these scents linger, but it did bring me some measure of comfort, as I had no other 'sense' of his presence. This lack of 'sense' worried me as a number of people, in their desire to say something helpful, had hinted that, as we had had such a good marriage, I must feel that Alan was still very close to me. It was not like that at all. There was only a deep void, a complete absence of anything I could hold on to. Even trying to remember his voice or visualize his face was difficult. He was gone, never to be touched, heard, seen or tasted in love again. He was lost to all but precious memory, yet catching that scent still comforts.

Inspired by the Bible

A fragrant act (Mark 14.3–9)

Thinking about it afterwards, she gave a little shiver of embarrassment. Never in her life could she have imagined herself doing such a thing. It was quite out of keeping with her usually shy and reserved nature, but today had been so different.

Life had been hard since Ezra died, leaving her alone and with their small son to support. Ezra had not thought to make provision for her in the event of his death. Well, why should he? He was a strong man. Who would have thought that he could be taken ill and die so suddenly? His three brothers all said how sorry they were, but, as she had a son, she couldn't expect one of them to marry her as the law would have allowed had she had been left childless. She couldn't blame them. They had enough trouble keeping their own families fed without taking on any more. She didn't beg or shame them into responsibility. She said she could manage and they weren't to worry. So they didn't – glad to be let off the hook. She managed as best she could, selling the few possessions she had left, gleaning in the fields and living off the charity of others, but it was grinding her down and she wasn't sure how much longer she could carry on.

It was Salome, who suggested that she join the group, for it was Salome who had found her crying early one morning by the well. Salome had been a good listener, drawing her into an embrace, until her story and the choking sobs had ceased. 'Why don't you come with us, perhaps just for a while, until you get back on your feet again?' she had suggested. 'We're just a group of women – I call us the Carpenter's Support Group,' she had said, laughing. 'Well, you should have seen them, absolutely no idea how to organize themselves or plan meals and Jesus is no better. Once he's preaching, he seems not to notice time or hunger.'

Salome was the mother of James and John, two of Jesus' disciples. She had told the story of how her two sons had been mending the nets with their father one day, when Jesus came along and asked them to join with him. 'I think Zebedee would have gone off with them as well, but I said someone had to be practical about this and look after the family business. "You stay at home," I said, "and I'll go and look after this lot." Talk about role reversal.'

The women all welcomed and accepted her without reservation or question. She particularly liked Mary of Magdala, a stunningly beautiful and flamboyant woman with a mass of long black curly tresses. Her hair was her crowning glory and she had the most expressive, sparkling eyes. When she looked at you, you were never sure whether she was laughing or teasing. Mary was the life and soul of the party. She would flash her eyes and say the most outrageous things and Jesus would laugh uncontrollably. It was rumoured that they might marry. Certainly, they were very close.

Being of a shy nature herself, she felt slightly uncomfortable with Jesus. Now and again she would be aware that he was looking directly at her and she would quickly look away. Somehow she felt too shy to look him in the eye.

Her son David, on the other hand, was completely uninhibited with Jesus, but then Jesus was great with the kids. He always took time to be with them, however tired he was. He told them stories, joked with them, played the clown and teased them lovingly. Jesus would make a good father, she thought.

She had awakened that day with an inexplicable feeling of unease. There was anxiety, too, among the others about the constant attention of the lawyers and priests. They were always at meetings, asking awkward questions. Jesus was not popular with them. He was openly critical about some of their practices and, clearly, they were hostile towards him, wanting to discredit him in the eyes of the people. Instead of being careful, Jesus was even more outspoken. Judas Iscariot seemed to be the only one in the group comfortable with this confrontation. She didn't care much for Judas. She felt his agenda was different from those of the rest. He seemed furtive, conspiratorial. His nationalistic pride, his passion to see the Romans overthrown and his impatience with Jesus' lack of action felt threatening.

Jesus' invitation to the house of Simon that evening seemed to offer them all a few hours of quiet respite from all the aggravation. Mind you, she didn't like Simon either, remembering only too well how, having received his offer of support following her husband's death, she discovered that it came at a price she was not willing to pay. Still, she wouldn't be seeing Simon as it was Jesus he had invited and, although some of the men folk would be going, the women would not be there.

After Jesus had left that evening, she walked down to the lakeside, taking with her the one possession that she could not bear to part with: a bottle of perfumed oil. It was worth a lot of money, but, even in the darkest times, she hadn't contemplated selling it. It had been part of her dowry. When Ezra died, she had anointed his body with some of the oil, but she had not broken the bottle and left it in the tomb, as was the custom. She had hidden it away, taking it out only at times of anxiety, when its scent seemed to offer her the strength and comfort that had been lost together with the man she loved.

Sitting by the lake, listening to the water ripple along the shore, she had hoped for some peace, but the abandoned fishing boats, like dark menacing hills, stark against the fading light of the night sky, and distant voices, like traitors' whispers, felt threatening and did nothing to relieve her sense of anxiety. Something was not right. It was a totally irrational feeling and she knew it, but, somehow, she had to see for herself – see that Jesus was safe. Clutching the bottle, she ran back into the village – the lights of Simon's house and the chatter of voices somehow beckoning her on. She didn't know what she was going to do, but knew that she had to do something. Looking back, the next few minutes were like a dream, one that she would remember in every detail for the rest of her life. Breathless with exertion, unable to speak, she burst in on the group and stood, looking for Jesus. All noise ceased and for a moment no one moved. All eyes were on her. In that moment, it seemed that her world was shocked into stillness. Suddenly it was clear. This was her one chance to offer her love and support, to let him know that she understood.

The bottle with its long neck to drip out the precious perfume drop by drop was too slow for her needs and so, in one swift movement, she broke it, allowing the contents to cascade in an avalanche of love.

It went ***everywhere*** – over Jesus' head, dripping down over his eyes, nose and beard, splashing on to the table and food, even reaching others in its journey of fragrance, finally to drip pools on the floor.

There was a unified gasp of horror from the guests and then the verbal abuse:

'What does she think she's doing?'

'Get her out of here!'

'What a waste!'

'Thousands could have been fed with the money that could have been raised from selling that perfume.'

'Are you mad, you stupid, stupid woman?'

She heard the words of censure, but she was not listening. She was looking directly at Jesus, seeing only gratitude in his eyes.

By now others were up on their feet, trying forcibly to remove her.

'Leave her alone!' Jesus' words rang out above the rabble. 'Don't get angry with her. She has done something really special. There will always be poor people, and you can show kindness to them whenever you wish, but I won't always be here. She has done what she could. She has anointed me as if for my burial and, I'll tell you this: wherever the good news is proclaimed in the whole world, what she has done will be told in memory of her.'

Suddenly, embarrassment overcame her and she ran out of the room, leaving the mess of her action for others to deal with. Turning the corner, she almost bumped into Judas Iscariot, striding off in the opposite direction. He had made his choice, as she had hers. She had released her fragrant love. She had *given* her silver. He had released his anger and disappointment and would *receive* silver for doing so.

Inspired by a memory

Remembering Brian

Some years ago, I used to go to the local primary school to play the piano for assemblies and singing sessions. In between these activities, I was given the task of hearing some of the children read, particularly those who were having a bit of a struggle. Brian was such a child. He came from a large, disadvantaged family. His parents found him a bit of a handful. If there was trouble, Brian always seemed to be in the centre of it. He was one of those lovable children, bright in a special way. He was sensitive and kind to others. Although often other children were unkind to him, he never seemed to bear a grudge. I felt that, whatever life threw at him, he would be a survivor. He was like a rubber ball, always bouncing back.

One day, as Brian turned the page in the Peter and Jane book we both found extremely boring, he looked up at me, sniffed and said, 'Cor, Mrs Bristow, you don't 'arf smell nice.'

'Thank you, Brian,' I said.

'Yes,' he went on, 'even when you're not in the room, I can smell that you've been there.'

I was touched by his comment and it made me remember the story of the anointing and the fact that the scent would have lingered for days on Jesus, in the house and maybe on others. A fragrant memory.

Relaxation and meditation exercise

Soothing balm

Preparation

Have an essential oil burner available as you reflect today. Choose an essential oil that you enjoy and has good associations for you. If you do not have a burner, you could put a few drops of essential oil on a tissue or handkerchief and place it where you can smell it during your time of reflection and meditation. If you are unsure what oil to use, you could try cedarwood, rosewood, lavender or rose. They are all helpful in creating a calm and peaceful atmosphere and are the oils most often used as an aid to meditation.

Alternatively, if you have a cold, you might like to use eucalyptus, which is not only good for cold and sinus problems but also helpful if you are feeling very tired. Try ylang ylang if you are feeling anxious or low, ginger for bronchitis and rheumatism, or tea tree for minor ailments.

You may like to play some quiet music as a background to the following meditation, otherwise just use the silence.

The exercise

Find a comfortable, quiet place and sit or lie back.

Shut your eyes and, slowly and gently, breathe in through your nose and out through your mouth. Be aware of the rhythm of your breathing.

Think about the 'inner' you, the amazing creation that you are. Think of your heart and lungs, which work ceaselessly every second of your life without your having to do anything about it.

Is there any part of your body that is hurting or aching? Concentrate for a few moments on that area as you breathe gently in and out. If you are feeling tense or anxious about anything, gently rub your hands together. In doing so, you are inadvertently massaging the solar plexus zone where so much tension is stored. The solar plexus is a network of nerve endings found behind the stomach. When we are nervous or anxious they become tense, giving rise to the expression 'a knot in my stomach'. Rubbing or wringing our hands relieves that tension.

When you feel relaxed, recognize that you are in the presence of God and, as you would with a good friend, share those things you want to share – concerns, joys, fears. Speak them in your mind or voice them out loud.

Then, allow some time of quiet and, as you breathe in, breathe in the love of God. God's own presence.

When you are ready, open your eyes and just sit quietly for a few more moments, taking in your surroundings and entering back into the reality of the day.

Worship material

Sweet memories – interactive Bible study

Preparation

Prepare a display with a length of red and a length of white material laid on the floor or a table. On this place a jug with red wine or blackcurrant juice or squash and plates of fruit, figs, dates, olives, some fingers of cheese and pitta bread.

Place at the edge of the display a bowl containing plain water that is large enough for people to dip their hands into. (Have two bowls if your group is large.) Also place there a small towel and a jug or bottle into which a quantity of olive oil and some drops of rose essential oil have been added.

Begin with some Jewish dance music, such as Hava Naguila, Horah and Zemer Atik (this can be found on many CDs of world music featuring music from Israel). Also, play Ma Naavou, for example, after the story has been read.

The event

As you welcome people to this interactive Bible study, invite them to wash their hands in the water before gathering around the display.

Read the story of the woman who anointed Jesus, as described in either Mark 14.3–9 or Matthew 26.6–13).

Invite people to think of an aroma or scent that has a special memory for them. What is the connection? Is it a happy memory? Is it associated with a time of sadness? Then ask them to share this with the person next to them or in a small group. For example, 'I cannot bear the smell of … because …' and 'I love the smell of … because …'.

Now have someone read the story given at the beginning of this chapter, topping and tailing it with some music, fading it in and out as appropriate.

Ask people to imagine themselves as guests at the meal to which Jesus was invited. If this can be dramatized, so much the better. Encourage people to think themselves into the part by describing the room, what people might be wearing, the sorts of conversations that might be going on. Again, you might like to encourage them to chat with a neighbour, asking questions such as, 'What is your name?', 'Where do you come from?', 'Have you met Jesus before?', 'What do you think about Simon's miraculous cure from leprosy?'

At the point in the story where Mary pours the oil over Jesus' head, pour out the scented oil from the jug or bottle into the bowl or bowls and stir it in.

At the end of the story, after the music has faded down, have a few moments of silence. Then, invite people to take food from the display and, in pairs or small groups, consider some or all of the following questions, while the food is shared.

Have you ever done something out of character because you felt you could not do otherwise, but, afterwards, wondered how you could have done such a thing?

Has anyone ever shown you an act of overwhelming generosity? Were you embarrassed by it?

Judas spoilt the moment of beauty with his comment about wastefulness. Has this ever happened to you – a moment spoilt by someone's negativity?

Whose life do you fragrance?

Invite people to come forward and dip their fingers into the bowl, which now contains the oil and perfume mixed in, and anoint their hands as the following Psalm of anointing is read.

Psalm of anointing

Anoint me, gracious God, with the oil of your grace
  that I may be a channel of your love to others.
Anoint my head, God of wisdom,
  so that my thinking and dreaming may be wise and loving.
Anoint my eyes, God of vision,
  that I may recognize you in the face of my sisters and brothers.
Anoint my ears, God of earthquake, wind and fire,
  that listening, I may hear the still small voice of justice and hope.
Anoint my lips, God whom language cannot describe or contain,
  that I may speak your words of comfort to those in distress.
Anoint my hands, God of compassion, who touched people others avoided,
  that I may hold out my hands to those in need.
Anoint my feet, pilgrim God, who travels through history with us,
  that I may leave familiar and comfortable places to risk new journeys with you.
Amen

Alternatively, you could use the following poem, Wasteful loving, here or at some other point in the programme. Songs or hymns could also be included if desired.

Wasteful loving

We are called to be risktakers.
Not for us the safety and security of the acceptable,
the tried and tested.
Not for us the careful measured dripping of love and passion,
but a reckless spilling of empathy,
breaking our complacency and inspiring us to give our all.

We will know that this we must risk:
to spill our love wastefully,
freeing it to cascade into the hidden crevices
of lost hope and despair,
finding its own level to work its healing balm.

It will be costly and sometimes our hearts will be broken,
our dreams will be smashed.

People will question our sense of direction,
challenge our motives
and test our confidence in things that cannot be quantified.

The words of censure will be there:
what a waste,
what a waste of time, resources, money and energy.

They will call us impetuous, emotional, silly, overextravagant
and tell us there are more deserving causes,
more important things to get fired up about.

We are called to be risktakers
for today and for the future.
To waft the aroma of sweet memory,
flowering in new areas of need.
One cannot happen without the other.
In the memory is a dying,
giving way to new visions hitherto undreamed of.

We are risktakers for the future.
Not always comfortable,
but then, why should we expect to be?

We will have done what we could,
risked for the sake of love
and the fragrance of the action will never be lost,
even if in the eyes of the world it has been wasted.

Rosemary for remembrance – a service of remembrance

Preparation

Make a display, on the floor or a low table, with room for people to sit in a circle around it or, if this is not practicable, use a table in a place that can be seen by everyone and reached easily, with space to move around it.

Have three coloured pieces of cloth to lay on the floor or drape over the table – one brown, one green and one a stone/dark brown colour. Lay the green and brown together and place the other one running down between them to weave like a path. Stand a few bare branches, either in a container or fixed with stones or clay, to signify a tree. Lay some autumnal-coloured leaves together with a pile of stones. There should be some large stones as well as others small enough to hold in the hand. Place four autumnal-coloured candles at intervals on the display to complement the fabrics.

You will also need:

- a small jug of olive oil with enough drops of rosemary essential oil added for the fragrance to be noticed when the oil is poured out
- felt-tip pens or pencils
- a large bowl
- a basket filled with leaf-shaped cut-outs in autumnal colours.

All of these are to be placed at either end of the display.

As well as three readers, you will need someone designated to light the candles at the appropriate time.

Here are some suggestions for music:

- Karl Jenkins, *The Armed Man: A Mass for Peace* and *Crossing the Stone*
- Coope Boyes and Simpson, 'Only Remembered', from *Funny Old World*
- Theme music from the film *Ladies in Lavender* by Nigel Hess
- Second Movement of Mendelssohn's 'Italian' Symphony No. 4
- Taizé, 'Jesus, remember me'
- John Rutter, *Requiem* and I will lift up mine eyes unto the hills, 'Pie Jesu' and 'The Lord is my Shepherd'.

The event

Have some quiet music playing as people enter, such as Crossing the Stone *or the* 'Italian' Symphony.

Leader: We gather together today to remember loved ones who have died. We give thanks for their lives and recall what they meant to us, tell their stories and refresh their memory by saying their names once more.

A few moments of silence while music continues, then fade music out.

Leader: Be still *(pause)*
be still and know *(pause)*
be still and know that I am *(pause)*
be still and know that I am God *(pause)*

Light one of the candles.

Reader 1: *(Reads Psalm 8.1–4.)*
What are human beings that you are mindful of them?

Reader 2: What are we? Physically, we are made up of 83 per cent water, plus a few metals and minerals, but that is not all we are! That is merely the shell containing within it a complex human being with the capacity to love and hate, to laugh and cry, to feel empathy and disgust, to be creative and to be destructive.

Also within each of us is a pearl of priceless treasure – God – and God is love.

Reader 3: *(Reads Psalm 139.1–6. The second candle is lit.)*

Reader 1: *(Reads Psalm 139.7–12. The third candle is lit.)*

Reader 2: *(Reads Psalm 139.13–18. The fourth candle is lit.*

Leader: Take a pebble from the display and write the name of the person or persons you wish to remember today. Hold the pebble and feel it become warm in your hands as you reflect on the person whose name you have written.

Play accompanying music – John Rutter, Pie Jesu' – Blessèd Lord Jesus, grant them rest. Blessèd Lord Jesus, grant them eternal rest.

Leader: Trees nurture and sustain themselves in a cycle of change. When two trees stand close together, sharing the same earth, water source and weather, some of their roots and branches intertwine, although they still remain as two separate trees, complete in themselves. However, if one tree dies or is cut down, it tears away some of the roots and branches of the other. The remaining tree can survive, repair and live on, but without the other its landscape and vista changes. It is a whole new scene.

With the loss of a loved one, your landscape will have changed, allowing you to view things from a different perspective, which is not necessarily negative, just different – a new horizon with other opportunities and different paths to pursue.

Play music – John Rutter', I will lift up mine eyes unto the hills.

Leader: Rosemary is the herb of remembrance.

I invite you to place your stone in the bowl provided in the display and pour a little of the oil of rosemary over it as you say the name you have written on it. You may wish to say one or two words about the person you are remembering – Paul was a great encourager, Mary was a special friend to me, for example – but words are not necessary. Just do what's right for you.

There will be silence while this takes place and then, when everyone who wishes to has participated, there will be a song/music.

Play music – Coope Boyes and Simpson, 'Only Remembered', *or Taizé,* 'Jesus, remember me' *or some other piece of your choosing.*

Leader: Picture a tree in autumn – its branches heavy with maturing fruit. In order to conserve its energy, the sap lowers in the tree. In their dying, the leaves change, taking on vibrant autumnal colours, and, as they fall to the ground, they slowly become the humus, which provides nourishment for future growth. Nothing is lost or wasted. It is the cycle of life.

Reader 3: *(Reads John 13.34.)*

Leader: Take a leaf as you leave to remind you that love is not lost. Like the autumn tree, letting go of its dying leaves, we too let go of the one who was for us the bearer of that love and whom we loved. We can be sure that they are safe in God's keeping and the memory of that love will never be lost or defeated, but lives on in the lives of those who are left, to nourish and sustain us.

Be still *(pause)*
be still and know *(pause)*
be still and know that I am *(pause)*
be still and know that I am God *(pause)*

Play music to leave to from the selection suggested earlier under 'Preparation' or a piece of your own choosing.

Activity

Hand massage for someone housebound or in hospital

Essential oils need to be mixed with a base or carrier oil – 3 drops to 10 ml – before applying to the skin. Buy the base or carrier oil when you buy your essential oil.

Try to get your oils from an accredited practitioner or a reputable chemist or healthfood shop. Never buy cheap oils – you get what you pay for and they will probably have little therapeutic value.

When visiting elderly or sick people, take a little bottle of ready-mixed base or carrier and lavender oil as a gift. Before you enter the ward or room, rub a couple of drops into the palm of your hand. As you greet the person, the scent will waft towards them, arousing their interest. That is your opportunity to offer to gently rub their hand and perhaps also give them a hand massage. It will relax you both and help you to communicate without the need for words.

However enthusiastic *you* may be, make sure that the recipient of your massage is happy to have this done. If not, simply leave the bottle of oil with them and suggest that they might like to put some on a handkerchief or tissue and place it under their pillow. Don't pressurize them. They may still like you to hold their hand and rub in a little hand cream.

Before massaging, remove any rings.

For a massage to be successful, your own hands need to be relaxed and ring-free. The whole of your hand should make contact with the other person, not just your fingertips. Think palm!

Once contact has been made, one hand at least should always remain in contact with the area you are working on.

Deep stroking is known as effleurage. It is a smooth, firm and fairly slow movement towards the heart, followed by a light, relaxed return to the starting point.

Follow the steps below for an enjoyable hand massage.

1. Effleurage the hand and lower arm. Only apply pressure when you are massaging upwards in the direction of the heart.
2. Gently flex, extend and rotate the wrist.
3. Massage the wrist bones making small circular movements.
4. Circle your thumbs as you move up the inner forearm.
5. Circle your thumbs between the metacarpals (the bones that you feel on the top of the hand running from the fingers to the wrist).
6. Turn the hand over and open it up, smoothing and stretching out the fingers so that the palm is flat and the fingers outspread. Make firm thumb circles over the palm.
7. Massage each finger in turn, working from the palm to the tip, away from the heart.
8. Effleurage the hand and lower arm.
9. Hold the hand between both of yours in a 'hand sandwich' for a moment to finish, making maximum contact.

(As taught by Penny Price)

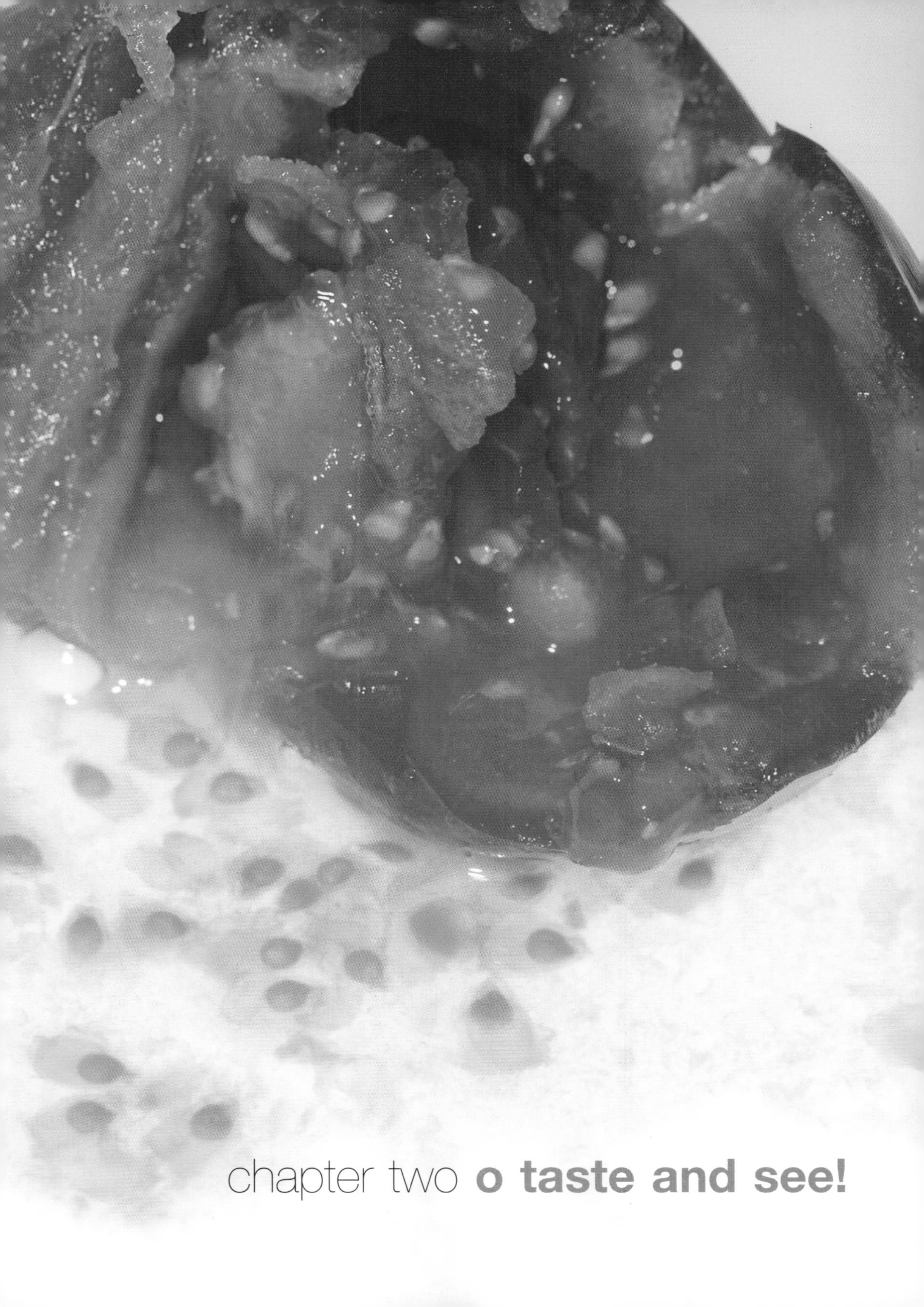

chapter two **o taste and see!**

‘How sweet are your words to my taste, sweeter than honey to my mouth!’

– Psalm 119.103

chapter two
o taste and see!

Food, as well as being vital for our very existence, is intended for our pleasure. Unlike other creatures, which may have a limited number of food sources, humans have a whole diverse range of foods to enjoy and, in order that we can do so, we have a very complicated taste system. On the tongue, we have about 10,000 taste buds, each of which contains between 50 and 100 receptor cells, and coming out of every receptor cell is a tiny taste hair that identifies the food chemicals in saliva. When these hairs are stimulated, they send nerve impulses to the brain. Each taste bud detects the five primary tastes.

There is a very strong social element to eating. We have special meals to celebrate and mark the significant events in our lives and we invite others to come and share them with us – baptisms, birthdays, weddings, anniversaries and funerals.

We also know that our attitude affects our appetites. When we are feeling unwell or when we are sad, cross or grieving or even when we have fallen out with someone and a relationship has been damaged, these things often affect how we feel about food. We can't eat or we 'comfort eat' and it's not until things are put right that we can get back to eating properly. Eating disorders, such as anorexia and bulimia, appear to be far more prevalent today than years ago and may well have something to do with advertising and the images portrayed in the media of how we 'should' look, as they have a lot to do with people's sense of self-worth.

Inspired by the Bible

Abundant wine (John 2)

The party was going splendidly and, for a few moments, Mary felt that she could relax. As a long-time friend of the family, she had offered to help with the catering for the wedding and Jesus and his brothers and sisters had all been invited to join the celebration. She had been a little annoyed when he had asked if his friends might come along also as this had meant the stress of greater numbers to cater for, but that was Jesus for you – he wanted everyone to be included in the fun. She leaned back against a tree for a moment, watching, looking around, checking that everyone had food enough to eat and wine to hand. Her eye was trained to see when plates needed replenishing.

She wished that Jesus would find a nice girl to marry. He was 30 now and most of his friends had teenage children. She worried about him. What was he doing with his life?

Her eyes moved over to where the six stone water jars stood and she noticed a group of servants talking animatedly – what was going on, she wondered. Suddenly she was bumped out of her thoughts by the dancers. She smiled – Jesus was leading the dancing round the courtyard as musicians played a fast and lively tune. The swish and colour of party clothes circled before her eyes. Yes, it was all going really well. The dancers moved on and, as they did so, one of the servants came up to her.

'We have a problem,' he said. 'The wine has run out. What are we going to do?' Her first thought was that they had made a mistake. 'We can't have run out,' she said. 'The bridegroom made sure there was plenty.' A sudden twinge of guilt hit her as she wondered if it was Jesus' friends who had in fact made the difference. Peter especially was always ready for food and wine.

'Just a minute, I'll see what I can do. Don't say anything to anyone else for the moment.' Jesus will know what to do, she thought, and now is the time for him to demonstrate that.

She looked around for him. The dance was continuing, but he had dropped out, laughing and talking with some of his old school friends.

Without thinking twice, Mary rushed over to him. 'Jesus, I need a word' and, taking him by the arm, moved him away from his friends.

'They have run out of wine, what can we do?' She looked up at his face. It was red with embarrassment. Oh dear, she had done the unthinkable – she had shown him up in front of his friends. No self-respecting mother would interrupt her eldest son in that manner. He was clearly put out! 'So,' he said, 'what's it got to do with me? It's not my problem. You're the one helping with the catering. Go and get some more from a neighbour or buy some from Mr Cohen at the wine bar.'

'Jesus!' she whispered through clenched teeth. 'Please help – I know you can find a way. I don't want to worry the bridegroom with this and there's no more money – it was all budgeted for very carefully. Perhaps if your friends hadn't come as well, this wouldn't have happened,' she added in irritation.

'Don't be silly, Mum, that's a ridiculous suggestion. Look, I'm not ready for this,' he protested, 'I'm just here to enjoy myself.'

'Please, Jesus, just for me?' she said, squeezing his arm and hoping to seduce him into action. She could tell by his face that it wasn't going to work.

'Oh, sometimes I wonder about you!' she exclaimed and, shaking her head, swiftly turned and walked back to the waiting servant.

'Now then,' she said to the man, 'I'm sure my son Jesus will help. Just be prepared to do whatever he asks of you.'

She hoped she hadn't overstepped the mark. She knew her son, but sometimes it seemed that he needed a push in the right direction. She just hoped she hadn't pushed too hard this time.

Mary pretended to busy herself with clearing empty plates and offering more food around. She heard someone call out for more wine and, looking up, she noticed Jesus over by the water jars, clearly, but unobtrusively, giving instructions.

'Just coming,' came the servant's response to a further call. It appeared to Mary that they were taking water out of the pots and putting it into the wine flagons. Surely they were not watering down what was left of the wine? She moved over to where John, the bridegroom, sat with some of his relatives, a tray of food in her hand. 'It's a wonderful party, Auntie Mary – thank you so much for all you've done,' he said. Mary smiled back at him, but her smile was made wider by hearing a voice shouting from the other side of the room, 'Hey, John, this wine is superb – how come you've kept the best until now?'

Phew! The disaster had been averted and the humiliation of the bridegroom avoided. Jesus had done something, quietly and gently, making no great demonstration of his skills. Secretly Mary wished that she could have boasted about her clever son, but she knew not to, as it was not his custom to boast. No one knew what had happened, apart from herself, Jesus and the servant. For the guests, nothing special had happened – all they noticed was that this wine tasted even better than the last. The party just continued without a hitch.

Later, at home, Mary asked Jesus about the water jars. 'Tell me,' she said. 'Each of those jars contained about 30 gallons of water. Did you turn *all* the contents into wine, all 180 gallons, or just what was transferred into the flagons?'

He looked at her and then said, smiling, 'What do you think?'

'Knowing you and your generosity, *all* of it!' she said.

'Let's just say, they'll be enjoying the celebrations for a little longer yet,' and, with a wink, Jesus left the room.

Inspired by a memory

Taking tea

I sat cross-legged on the concrete floor, trying to accustom my eyes to the darkness. Even on the sunniest of days, these small, one-roomed dwellings – the homes of families of workers on the tea estates – are dark and dismal, for there are no windows and only one door. Smoke billows from the open fire in one corner of the room by the door and threatens to choke those unaccustomed to the fumes. In this estate house, apart from a small double bed and a little glass-fronted cabinet holding the few precious family items, the room is bare. I count the number of people coming in and discover that 30 have crowded into this small room for the prayer meeting. It is an occasion for the whole community to attend – Buddhists, Hindus and Christians all squashed together. An oil lamp in one corner bathes us in a warm red glow as we sing and pray together.

I learned that Anna, the hostess, is a tea picker and, through an interpreter, she told me that, on this particular tea estate, only women are allowed to pick the tea, and not only is it the lowest-paid of all the jobs but also the women are not allowed to progress to another area of work.

The women work in groups and, each morning, are allotted an area in which to work. In order to earn the full wage for the day, they are required to pick a certain weight in leaves. If their total falls below the quota, however little that might be, their pay is reduced by half. Some of the women are able to pick quickly, the younger ones more nimble on the hillsides. Some are older and slower. In order that, at the end of the day, as many as possible earn a full day's money, they will often share out the surplus of those who have picked more among those who do not have enough in their baskets.

At the end of the meeting, a cup of tea and a biscuit were offered. This was generous hospitality indeed – coming from people who pick and process the tea leaves, but are so poorly paid for their labour – offered to someone who, in future, will think carefully about the cost, in human terms, of the cup that cheers. A reminder to us all that the very least we can do is make sure that we buy only fairly traded tea and coffee and, indeed, other products.

Reflective exercise

Food for the world

Preparation

With your morning coffee or tea, treat yourself to a biscuit or cake (using fairly traded items or ingredients) and eat it slowly, savouring the flavours and textures – just enjoy it!

Perhaps you might like to invite friends and neighbours to join you this morning for coffee and reflection.

Have a small bowl of rice and a world map on the table in front of you. If you have access to Christian Aid or Oxfam publications or the *New Internationalist*, you may find it helpful to refer to them today. Using the internet, you can also check their websites for up-to-date information and stories.

Bible passage

Read Amos 5.21–24 and reflect on what this means for us today.

Reflections

Each country has its basic food – be it rice, bread or yams – but, for many, even the most basic food is scarce and there is certainly very little variety available. Looking at the map, identify places in the world where people go hungry and then place a few grains of rice on as many places as possible. Sit quietly for a while, naming these places in your mind and bringing them before God in your thoughts.

As you look at the map and the countries you have identified, consider and reflect on:

- what things add to the problem of lack of food and resources – climate, wars, multinational companies, oppressive governments or greed

- reflect on how you feel about the initiatives that have been taken following the Make Poverty History campaign – what else can we do?

Perhaps you might like to take one of the grains of rice from the map each day and replace it with a coin or message or prayer of commitment.

This could also be used as a small group activity.

Food glorious food

For those who plant it.

Food glorious food.
For those who produce it.

Food glorious food.
For those who market it.

Food glorious food.
For those who transport it.

Food glorious food.
For those who sell it.

Food glorious food.
For those who can buy it.

Food glorious food.
For those who will share it.

Food glorious food.
For those who are denied it.

Food glorious food.
From God who provides it.

Hot food and cold food,
sweet food and sour food,
spicy tastes and bland tastes,
colourful and crunchy,
soft and munchy,
creamy food and lumpy,
slippery and velvety.
So much variety.
Thank God who provides it!
Food glorious food.

Worship material

Remember me

This can be used as a reflective service for the whole church, with people being invited to share their own stories of meals taken, or, alternatively, it can be acted out as a drama within a worship service.

Preparation

Place a long table and five chairs round it, either at the front of the church or down the centre, and lay a white cloth over it. Set four places at the table, leaving one place empty. Each setting should have a placecard with a dinner candle and a sprig or two of rosemary.

You will need five people to play the characters and a narrator. The characters are:

- Zacchaeus
- Simon, cured of leprosy
- Mary, Jesus' mother
- Mary, Martha's sister
- Judas Iscariot.

Choose some music, such as a Hebrew melody, perhaps, or the 'Sabbath Prayer' from *Fiddler on the Roof.* Also, between each person speaking and as they light their candle, be prepared to play or sing two phrases of 'Jesus, remember me' from *Laudate*, the music of Taizé.

Here are some other suggestions for hymns or songs that you might like to use if required:

- 'O taste and see', *Love from Below*, Wild Goose Publications
- 'Let us break bread together on our knees', *Rejoice and Sing* and others
- 'Let us talents and tongues employ', *Rejoice and Sing*
- 'We meet as friends at table', *Piece together Praise* by Brian Wren.

The event

Play some music as the characters enter and take their places at the table.

Narrator: Many of the gospel stories and parables are centred on food. Jesus was always sharing meals with people, many of whom were considered social outcasts by the religious leaders of the day. However, it seems that there were no conditions placed on Jesus' acceptance of hospitality, but usually the disciples came along, too! Perhaps this tells us that when we invite Jesus to sit with us, his friends come as well. We can't entertain Jesus in isolation. The poor, needy, despised and sidelined are the friends he brings with him and he insists they share in the hospitality. People came into a relationship with Jesus around the meal table, where they suddenly found that he was giving of himself and supplying their need for spiritual nourishment. 'I am the bread of life,' said Jesus.

Around this table are people who all shared meals with Jesus. For each of them, it was a very special occasion.

Zaccheus stands and lights his candle and holds his sprig of rosemary.

Zachaeus: My name is Zacchaeus and I remember.

Yes, I know what you are thinking – nasty little man, up a tree, a tax-collector who everyone despised and nobody wanted to invite into their home, but you'd be wrong. Jesus actually asked to come to my home and share food. I nearly fell out of the tree in which I was hiding. I was really worried, though, because I thought Jesus would condemn me in front of the whole crowd as everyone was looking up at me, but he simply asked for my hospitality.

That meeting completely changed my life. Over food, we talked about what I was doing – not just that I collected taxes, but, like so many other tax-collectors, I was adding on to the original figure and demanding extra money, lining my own pockets in the process. I was taking advantage of people, who might have gone without food to feed the family in order to pay me. No wonder I had no friends except other tax-collectors!

Jesus didn't seem to condemn or judge me or tell me what a bad lot I was. He just enabled me to see what I was doing and, once I was faced with that … well, things changed for me. I felt that I had to do more than just give back what I had taken and now I don't have a job and I have no money. I don't know what I shall do. I am trusting that something will turn up, but I know I have done the right thing and, somehow, I feel like I can lift my head up high and walk tall.

Narrator: So let us remember all those who have recently become followers of Jesus and what that has meant for them:

- those who have lost their jobs or felt that they could no longer, in all conscience, stay in the job they were doing
- those who have lost friends
- those trying to lead a different life and those who support them.

Pause.

Narrator: Jesus is the bread of life

All: and all have a place at the table.

Sing or play 'Jesus, remember me', from Laudate, *Taizé.*
Simon stands and lights his candle and holds his sprig of rosemary.

Simon: I am Simon and I remember.

I used to be known as Simon the Leper. No one wants to associate with someone who has the stigma of leprosy. The very word drives fear into the hearts of those who hear it and, for the sufferer, it's a living death. So, like you, Zacchaeus, I was shunned by people, but for a different reason. I was desperate.

Jesus made me a whole person and, suddenly, life was good again – friends returned and I was included in the life of the village. Anyway, to celebrate, I decided to have a party and invite my old friends and I thought it would be good to invite Jesus, too, though I wouldn't normally invite a carpenter to dine with me – he was not in my social class, you understand – but he was a bit of a celebrity and I thought it would give a certain interest to the evening, the novelty factor.

Things were going very well, I thought, and then, suddenly, it all went pear-shaped. Seemingly from nowhere, this woman gatecrashed the party and broke a whole bottle of perfume over Jesus' head. It was so embarrassing. I don't know who she was or where she had come from, but, I tell you, I got the servants to bundle her out pretty quick. Jesus just sat there, with all this highly perfumed oil spilling down over his head and shoulders – there was such a mess, in more ways than one. The servants brought some towels and tried to mop up the worst of it. After the initial anger and embarrassment, one or two started to smile and laugh – well, in some ways it was so funny to see him sitting there, but, as Judas pointed out, what a waste of good money.

Then there was another shock as Jesus came to the defence of the woman. He pointed out, to my shame, that she had done what I had failed to do. She had anointed him with perfume, whereas I had not even washed his feet as a good host should.

I felt so ashamed after all that Jesus had done for me and it made me realize that I hadn't shown him even the basic courtesy.

Narrator: So let us remember all those who are excluded:

- because of their gender or sexual orientation
- because of their race, colour or creed
- because of their social standing.

Pause.

Narrator: Jesus is the bread of life

All: and all have a place at the table.

Sing or play 'Jesus, remember me', from Laudate, *Taizé.*

Mary stands and lights her candle and holds her sprig of rosemary.

Mary: I am Mary, Jesus' mother. Of course I remember many happy family meals – the children's birthdays, Passover, Hanukkah and, especially, Jesus' bar mitzvah. I remember, too, the time when he was invited to John's wedding in Cana and he took all his new friends and the wine ran out. I remember he was so reluctant to get involved because he said he was having a good time enjoying himself and it really wasn't his problem, but I kept on at him until he relented and, my, the wine tasted good!

There were sad times, too, especially when Joseph died and there was an empty place at the table, and after Jesus had left home to start his ministry, when there was another empty place. I used to worry then in case he wasn't getting enough to eat, so sometimes, when they were in the area, I would take them all some home-cooked food. I wasn't around at the last meal he had – the one we now know was his last supper with his disciples – but I helped to prepare it. I just wonder what was going through his mind as he shared that time with his friends. Once in a while, John comes by and we have a meal together and we remember.

Narrator: So let us remember those who have an empty place at their table:

- because of the death of a loved one
- because there has been a family rift
- because someone is in hospital or care.

Pause.

Narrator: Jesus is the bread of life

All: and all have a place at the table.

Sing or play 'Jesus, remember me', from Laudate, *Taizé.*

Mary (Martha's sister) stands and lights a candle and holds her sprig of rosemary.

Mary: My name is also Mary. You remember, I am sure, Martha's sister Mary. Jesus often came to our house for meals when he was in the area. It was somewhere he could feel at home, relax and enjoy home cooking. We became his family, too. Martha is a marvellous cook but, oh dear, she gets in such a tizzy when we have visitors. She goes to endless trouble and wants everything to be just right. I know that Jesus would have been pleased just to have had bread and cheese, but, no, Martha had to make her best dishes for him. That was her way of expressing her love for him. Now me, well, I just wanted nothing more than to sit at his feet and listen to him talking. Martha had made her choice and I mine. The conflict came when she felt that I ought to have made the same choice as she had. I told her quietly not to fuss, but she did make me feel guilty. Then, not getting a response from me, she appealed to Jesus. I was so relieved to hear Jesus say, 'Mary has made her choice', but I could see that she was deeply hurt.

Now, of course, that time has gone – we no longer have the pleasure of his physical company – and I am so pleased that I made the choice I did, and I know Martha was pleased that she did her very best for his comfort. So, we were *both* doing the right thing. We had each made our choices with Jesus' best interests at heart.

Narrator: So let us remember those who have a ministry of hospitality:

- those who open their homes to others
- those who staff hostels for the homeless at Christmas
- those who give their time to listen to others.

Pause.

Narrator: Jesus is the bread of life

All: and all have a place at the table.

Sing or play 'Jesus, remember me', from Laudate, *Taizé.*

Judas stands and lights his candle and holds his sprig of rosemary.

Judas: Judas – that's my name. A name synonymous now with the word 'traitor'. You're wondering how it is that I can be invited to share food with these people. Perhaps it is because we all need to be reminded that we do things of which we are ashamed. That one split second in history, I made a mistake. I tried to force Jesus' hand, to make him act, to take up the sword and fight for what he believed. At the time, I thought there was nothing wrong with that. Many of you have pushed others into taking action by fighting wars or getting involved in conflict of one sort or another. History is littered with such moments. You believed in what you were doing: so did I. He knew what was in my mind, of course, and, instead of restraining me, he blessed me with the best portion of food during that last meal. It was the last supper for Jesus and the last for me also. I regretted what I'd done so bitterly, that I could not go on living. Perhaps the biggest mistake I made was not believing that I could be forgiven.

Narrator: So let us remember those who despair:

- those who, in a split second, made the wrong choice and live with the consequences
- those who are wrongly imprisoned
- those who take their own lives in despair
- those who cannot accept forgiveness
- those who cannot forgive themselves
- those whom the world makes into scapegoats.

Pause.

Narrator: Jesus is the bread of life

All: and all have a place at the table.

Sing or play 'Jesus, remember me', from Laudate, *Taizé.*

If desired, invite the congregation to share a story of a special meal, using the empty place setting and holding the sprig of rosemary while talking.

After each contribution, the Narrator could use the same form of responses and music as before.

Kitchen talk

Preparation

If possible, have some large jars or pots as props for the scene. Martha is sitting on a stool, peeling some vegetables, obviously upset, trying to hold back tears of frustration and anger. She is startled as Jesus appears.

The event

Martha: (Looks up at Jesus.)

Oh, I didn't see you there. I thought you were still in the courtyard with the others *(she starts to bustle about with pots and pans)*. I'm just putting the last few touches to the meal. There is so much to do I don't know quite where to begin.

Jesus: (Casually.)

So I see. Um, I just thought I would come and see what you were doing, you seemed a bit upset.

Martha: (Gives little nervous laugh.)

Upset? Why should I be upset? It's a lovely day. You are here and …

Jesus: You are cross with me, aren't you, Martha?

Martha: Of course not. Anyway, what right do I have to be cross with you, Jesus?

Jesus: Oh come on, Martha, of course you are. Stop pretending and acting the martyr. You're cross because I told you to stop fussing and wouldn't tell Mary to get up off her backside to come and help you in the kitchen.

Martha: (Turning round, unable to repress her anger.)

All right, then, yes, I *am* angry if you want to know, angry and hurt.

Jesus: (In a teasing manner.)

Ahh, the truth's coming out now.

Martha: Mary isn't the only one who wanted to sit by you and listen to your news. Do you think I wanted to hide away in the kitchen all by myself? I would have loved to have just sat myself down at your feet and listened to you speaking.

Jesus: Well, why didn't you then?

Martha: (Getting really angry.)

Well, *someone* had to get a meal ready, didn't they? Let's be honest, it's not as if you come by yourself – you always bring others with you and you know how much that Peter eats.

Jesus: (Smiling.)

Would you like me to tell him not to eat so much in future?

Martha: You will tell him no such thing! *(Pauses.)* Oh, I'm sorry, I'm hot and tired and just so hurt. I was simply trying to do my best for you – cooking the dishes you like, making sure you were comfortable, that the place was clean, there were fresh flowers and newly baked bread ready – and you didn't once say that what I was doing was good or thank me for my trouble. You just said I was making a fuss and Mary *(sarcastically)*, Little Miss Mary, sitting there looking as if butter wouldn't melt in her mouth, was doing the right thing.

Jesus: (Gently puts his hands on Martha's shoulders.)
Martha, Martha, I am so sorry. I didn't mean to hurt you. One of the reasons I love coming here is because your hospitality is so wonderful. I can be at home here. This is where I can relax in comfort, savour the things that most people take for granted. This is the one place where I don't have to be on my guard. It is really the only home I have! You, Martha, above anyone else, make that possible – the ministry of hospitality that you perform is one beyond price – and I thank you for it, but I shall not always be able to do this, Martha. I am not going to be around forever and there are things that I want to tell you all and share with you, and I am prepared to wait for my dinner in order that you, too, may have the opportunity to sit and talk with me. Come on now, let's join the others and let Peter wait for his great feast a little longer.

I cannot believe it!

Preparation

Two people are needed to take part in this dialogue. Levi could be setting a table for the meal, with a tablecloth, cutlery, dishes, bread and a bowl of fruit while he and Nat talk.

Levi: I cannot believe I am doing this.

Nat: Doing what?

Levi: Getting ready to have Jesus to dinner. You know who he is, don't you?

Nat: Only that he is one of these new religious teachers. I can't see what all the fuss is about. What is so special about this one?

Levi: *This* one stopped to talk to me and asked me to be one of his disciple group. That's what makes him so special. When was the last time anyone from the synagogue spoke to you or invited you to dinner? People with *leprosy* are treated better than tax-collectors! At least people feel sorry for them. I just can't believe that this is happening to me.

Nat: So you keep saying.

Levi: I was just sitting there, Nat, in my booth, trying not to be noticed. It was such a large gathering and I thought to myself, 'Keep your head down, Levi – he may be going to incite them to riot against the Roman authorities' and I would be literally a sitting target for any stone-throwing.

Nat: So what did he say to you, then, this Jesus?

Levi: Well, not much really. He just stopped talking and walked over to where I was sitting. I don't mind telling you that I came out in a cold sweat and I thought I'd had it. Then he just smiled at me. It was such a relief, because I thought he was going to denounce me, but he just held out his hand and said, 'So, what about it? Are you going to join me? I'd like to have your company.' I couldn't believe my ears.

Nat: What will this mean, do you think? Will you have to give up your job now? Leave the Guild of Tax-collectors? Go all holy and righteous?

Levi: I don't know, really. There are so many questions I want to ask Jesus, which is why I invited him round for this meal.

Nat: Huh! How did you persuade him to come? That is a real sign of friendship.

Levi: Well, actually, it wasn't difficult. I didn't have to persuade him at all. He said 'Yes' immediately and, not only that, he asked if he could bring his friends along, too. Apparently, it's common knowledge – if anyone invites Jesus to eat with them, they have to entertain his friends as well. All of them in this case.

Nat: Well, this is going to be an interesting meeting. How many Guild members have you invited?

Levi: Quite a few, so it's a good job the house is large enough. I do so want you all to meet him. I've never heard anyone say the sorts of things he says. Anyway, I can't stand around talking, I must make sure that all is ready.

(Sound of someone knocking at the door.)

That must be him. Oh dear, I cannot believe this is happening to me.

(Offstage, a voice is heard.)

Voice: Are you there – it's me, Jesus. Can I come in?

(Freeze the scene and hold for a few moments of silence.)

Food for the soul

Dear God,
isn't your creation wonderful!
And your provision for us so prolific,
far exceeding what we need.
Good things you shower on us, with a reckless generosity
that takes our breath away,
spilling such a feast of tastes and textures, shapes and colour before us
until our senses are sated and we can feast no more.
Our plate and cup are overflowing.

And, as if that were not enough, you give yourself to us
our sustenance and nourishment – our bread of life.

Generous God,
you provide enough and more for all your children.
Yet we are selfish with your generosity,
often unwilling to share with others what is also rightly theirs.
Forgive us our paucity of spirit, our meanness and our greed.
Give us the wisdom to use your gifts wisely,
so that all may have a share in your overflowing goodness.

Provider God,
food for our souls as well as our bodies.
May we so consume you that, as carriers of your love,
we may be the source of nourishment and energy
to those who can only dream of a feast.

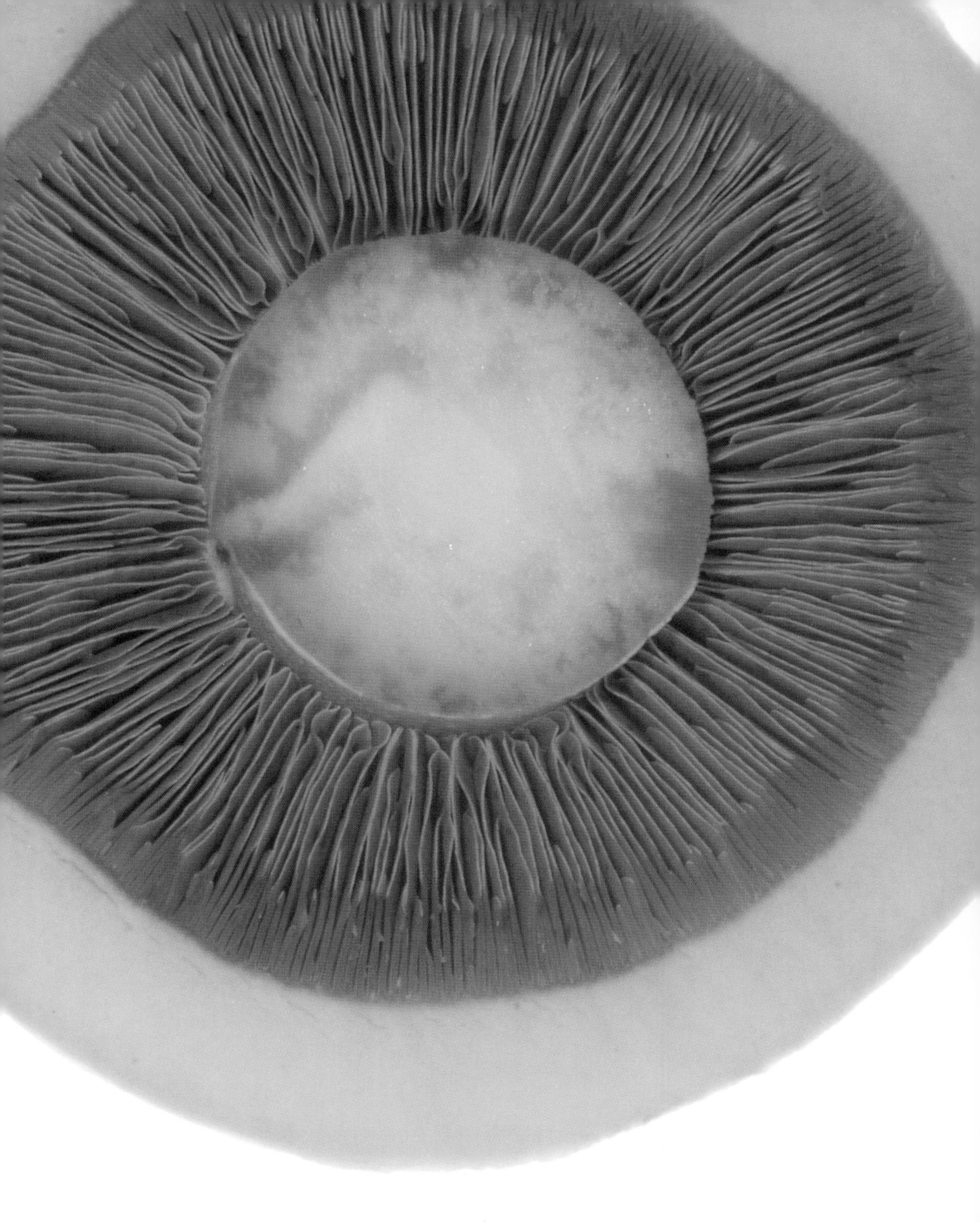

chapter three **seeing is believing**

**'We do not see things as they are.
We see things as we are.'**

– *Talmud*

chapter three
seeing is believing

How do we see? For most of us, it is through our eyes – those two amazing organs that act as mirrors on the world for us – but it is the optic nerve that transmits impulses to the brain and it is the brain which makes sense of what we see. In fact, it is such a complex system that nearly a third of the entire brain is devoted to vision.

How do I know that everyone else sees what I see? If you ask two different people to describe someone or something, the chances are that the detail will be different. Is *my* green colour the same as everyone else's? Can I be sure that what I have described is accurate, true in every detail?

What about those people who have lost their sight or were born without sight? How do they 'see'? Some would say that they 'see' through touch and a heightening of their other senses and the window of their imagination. As well as seeing literally, we 'see' beyond the object, our environment and the people around us.

Inspired by the Bible

Who are you looking for? (John 20)

She wasn't sure what she felt any more. Emptiness, confusion, physical pain, fear – all those certainly and, yes, she needed to admit it, anger, too. Just about every emotion had kept company with her through the dark hours since his death and now, exhausted by it all, she had come to be near him for the last time, to say her own farewell, although even that seemed denied her now.

It was still dark when she left the house that morning and, shivering in the cold, fresh air of a new day yet to break, her senses suddenly became alive again and she was aware of the feel of the dewy grass around her feet, the sharp aroma of the garden shrubs – such a contrast to Friday and the smell of the city's rubbish dump, the site of execution, with its stink of rotting vegetation and the smell of fear and death. Yet, even there he had made a difference, as the scent of the perfume that she had so lovingly lavished on him a few days earlier still lingered, speaking its own message of sacrificial love, pervading the evil smell of corruption and betrayal.

Saturday had seemed the longest day of her life – a day of anxious waiting. They had tried their best to comfort one other, especially his mother, but what was there to say? It was all over. All that was left to them was the one last duty they could perform – to bury him properly. Nothing would ever be the same again.

Unable to sleep, they had spent the long hours going over and over the sequence of events that had led to his trial and death. It had all happened so suddenly. One minute he was being hailed as the Messiah, the next as a traitor. The eternal 'Why?' had been a frequent question and she was surprised at her own feeling of anger. How could they have all been so cowardly? How could they have let it happen? More surprisingly, perhaps, how could he, Jesus, have let it happen? Surely, of all people, he could have prevented it? He didn't even try to defend himself and no one else was prepared to speak for him. How awful it must have been, knowing that he was totally on his own, that everyone had deserted him in his hour of greatest need. Yet she, too, felt a small sense of betrayal. She had loved him, would have done anything for him and had been left desolate.

With tears still obscuring her vision, she bent forward for one final look into the tomb, surprised to see that already others were there. One spoke: 'Why are you crying?' 'Because they have taken Jesus away,' she had said, 'and I don't know where they have put him.' Turning away, so she did not have to answer any more of their questions – she came face to face with a man she took to be the gardener. As if clutching at a final straw, she asked him, 'Have you carried him away, moved the body of Jesus? Please, please, tell me where you have put him and I will tend to his body.' The man looked at her and said just the one word: 'Mary.' ... There was only one person who said her name quite like that. In that moment she saw ... and, shrieking out the word 'Master', she threw herself towards him as if to hug him. She wanted to hold him, to feel the warmth of his body, the beating of his heart, to touch him and make sure that this was no dream, he was alive again. The adrenaline was rushing to her head, making her incoherent with joy. He was alive, alive, and it was all going to be all right. They would all be back together again and life could continue as it had been. Suddenly, his words bit hard through her euphoria: 'Do not hold on to me, Mary, for I have not yet returned to the Father. Go instead and tell the others "I am returning to my God and your God." '

In that moment she saw also another truth. Things were not going to be the same as they were before. He was alive all right, but in a different way. He was not going to be confined any more to a particular place or time or belong only to a few. Now, everyone could have that special relationship that she had had with him. She mustn't hold him to herself, she must not cling to what was, but be open to what might be. This good news was for all.

Inspired by a memory

He said my name

In June 1967, I was returning to the home of my parents-in-law, where I had been staying, on and off, with our two small children, Stephen and Alison, since our evacuation from Biafra exactly a year before.

We had agreed before leaving Britain for Nigeria that if, as people predicted, a civil war broke out, I would return home with the children and Alan, my husband, would remain. Three months after arriving in Enugu, Eastern Nigeria, that is exactly what happened and Eastern Nigeria, under the leadership of General Ajuku, broke away, forming its own country – Biafra.

One night, with two hours' notice, the call came to evacuate women and children. I could take one suitcase. What would I pack? What was it going to be important to take? I realized that I was unlikely to see anything I left behind ever again. In the end, together with the necessary changes of clothes, I took the hymnbook Alan had given me at our wedding and the family photograph album. Well, not the album, we took the photos out so that they didn't weigh too much.

Having expected to be living in Nigeria for at least six years, we had sold our home and most of the furniture, shipping out with us just our personal and most treasured possessions and furnishings.

So it was that I, with many other mothers and children, returned to England.

During the next year, we lived a nomadic existence, moving around to different friends and family who offered us hospitality. Biafra was cut off from the outside world and contact with Alan was very sporadic. I had resigned myself to the fact that Alan was thousands of miles away and even that I might never see him again.

The front door of my parents-in-law's home in Reigate led straight in to the stairs, with two doors off to the left and right. As I opened the door on that particular day, my eyes went immediately to the top of the stairs and I saw what I thought was Derek, Alan's brother, standing there. I turned around to close the door and, as I did so, I heard the voice from the top of the stairs say my name – 'Stella'. Immediately I knew who it was – it was the way he said my name. This was not Derek, but Alan. We met somewhere halfway up or down the stairs and I cannot remember what we said in that moment of joy, except that I couldn't say much, for I was just clinging on to him, making sure that this was not a dream, but reality. He was back, he was alive and well, although incredibly thin. Things were never going to be the same again, though. It was going to be a different journey for us now.

Reflective exercise

Insight

A suitable place for this activity would be a quiet corner, perhaps where you can make a little focal point. Cover a table with a coloured cloth or piece of material, but initially nothing else. Have paper and pencil handy to jot down things that come into your mind. It may be that you could just sit by a window looking out into a garden or street. Take time to sit quietly for a moment and look carefully at what is around you.

Make sure you feel comfortable, then shut your eyes and take a few deep breaths. Most people breathe shallowly, from the chest. Try to breathe from the stomach – it is your stomach that should expand as you breathe in, not your chest. Observe the breathing of a baby to see exactly how to do it. If you bring the air right down into the lungs, the oxygen exchange is more efficient, causing the heart rate to slow down and the muscles to relax, hopefully engendering a feeling of calm. Breathe in through the nose, slowly, your stomach expanding, then breathe out through the mouth. Exhaling should take twice as long as inhaling.

With your eyes still closed, what do you 'see'? What images pass into your mind? Don't try to dismiss any of them, just acknowledge what comes. It may be that other sounds will intrude or become part of the images – that is OK. Take as much time as you want for this exercise and, if you fall asleep, so be it. It probably means that is what you need.

Think of your most treasured possessions. If you had to choose to keep only three, what would you choose? If these are moveable and small enough, put them on your table or write what they are on your piece of paper. Why are they important? What feeling or sense do they evoke in you?

Think about and reflect on any experience in your life where you have seen, perhaps just for a fleeting moment, signs of God's presence.

Think of a time when you saw a situation or an object in a totally different light. Was there ever a time when you struggled with an idea or thought or a puzzle – something you couldn't work out – when, suddenly, the penny dropped and everything fell into place or the problem was resolved?

Have you ever been in a situation where something totally unexpected has happened? How did you 'see' this and what significance did it have for you?

Read again the story of Mary in the garden and consider all the emotions associated with the story. Sadness, emptiness, loss, anger, anxiety, joy, relief, confusion. Remember a time when you have experienced these emotions. Does the memory remain with you? Has anything changed since that time? Are you still clinging on to anything that prevents you from moving on? Is it a good memory or a difficult one?

If you wish, you could have several reflective sessions, taking one feeling or emotion at a time.

Reflective exercise

A walk of seeing

Go for a walk, concentrating only on what you see. Look carefully at your surroundings. Don't attempt to touch or smell and try not to pay attention to the sounds around you – just look. Look at the detail, the colour and the shapes of things. If it is a familiar walk, what have you noticed that is different from previous times? Walk slowly and carefully, practising deep breathing as described above. This is easier to do if you are walking.

How do you see? Are there other ways of seeing than with your eyes, through touch and hearing, intuition?

Coming and going

They didn't understand,
how could they?

Each time he appeared it was for them miraculous, reunion with a beloved friend and teacher.
Each goodbye confirming they had come of age.
A new relationship now to forge,
no longer bound to place and time,
but a different way of being – part of them, within them,
yet available to all.
But for me, it caused such pain –
not as the pain that delivered him from my body,
nor the one that pierced my heart as I rocked his body in death.
Those little remembrances of what he had been to me,
a beloved son –
not that I had always understood him, of course.
Well, who can truly say that they know their children?

His ways at times were very strange to me,
even to believing him unwell and mentally unstable.
I tried to protect him – to take him home, to safety and stability.

But he rejected that – he rejected anything that sought to hold him, claim him.
But, coming and going like that,
each time the pain of parting was worse,
each time another death experienced.

And then, that last time,
when all was made known,
when the clouds of grief and pain were lifted from my eyes,
and I saw, and knew, and believed.

Worship material

Seeing is believing

Preparation

Drape a piece of white material over a low table making sure that it covers the table and legs. Stand on this a five-branched candlestick or five individual candles, to be lit later. Four of the candles should be of different colours, the centre candle being a white one.

You will also need a loaf of bread on a platter, some grapes, dates and a pottery jug of water with some goblets and a number of large pots or pitchers placed around the area with some cushions or small mats. Have, too, a basket or bowl containing tealights – enough for every member of the congregation.

Apart from the leader, you will need three other people to play the different parts.

For the music for Drama Part 1, 'Slave Children's Crusade' from *Indiana Jones and the Temple of Doom* has a very spooky feel and one can imagine the sound of a Roman army on the march.

For Drama Part 2, 'I know that my Redeemer liveth' from Handel's *Messiah* works well, but equally you could choose some other suitable music.

The event

Leader: None of the disciples believed in the risen Jesus until they saw him for themselves. They had seen him condemned to death and each one believed only when they had seen him after his death on the cross. It was first-hand experience. So, why are we surprised at Thomas? He was not there when Jesus appeared to the others, so why should he believe them? Remember, we know the end of the story – they did not. Thomas wanted more than just to 'see' – he needed to touch. Mary, though, was told not to touch. There's a difference – touching for sight and touching to cling on to what was.

There was a change in the relationship that was based not on physical but spiritual presence. We don't have to accept everything others say without question. Jesus did not ask that of Thomas. You cannot take on yourself someone else's experience – they have to prove themselves! In the end, maybe there is faith, which is about accepting, taking a risk, working with something as if you *had* 'seen' and believed it.

Drama Part 1

This part of the drama is played out of sight of the congregation.

The leader lights one of the candles (leave the centre one to be lit last) as music is played, then moves out of sight. Fade out the music and pause after 50 seconds or allow the music to run quietly under the drama, turning it up at the points suggested.

Voice 1: Peter, come in, come in and, yes, James and Andrew. Be quick all of you! Did anyone see you coming?

Voice 2: For goodness sake, put that lantern out, Nathaniel! Hurry up inside everyone!

Voice 3: Is Mary here and Philip?

Voice 1: Yes, all but Thomas. Let's get this door bolted.

Turn up the music for a few seconds, then pause after one minute for the Bible reading, which should be read unannounced as a continuation of the drama.

Leader: (Reads John 20.19–26.)

Play more music, for approximately 30 seconds, while the reader lights one of the coloured candles.

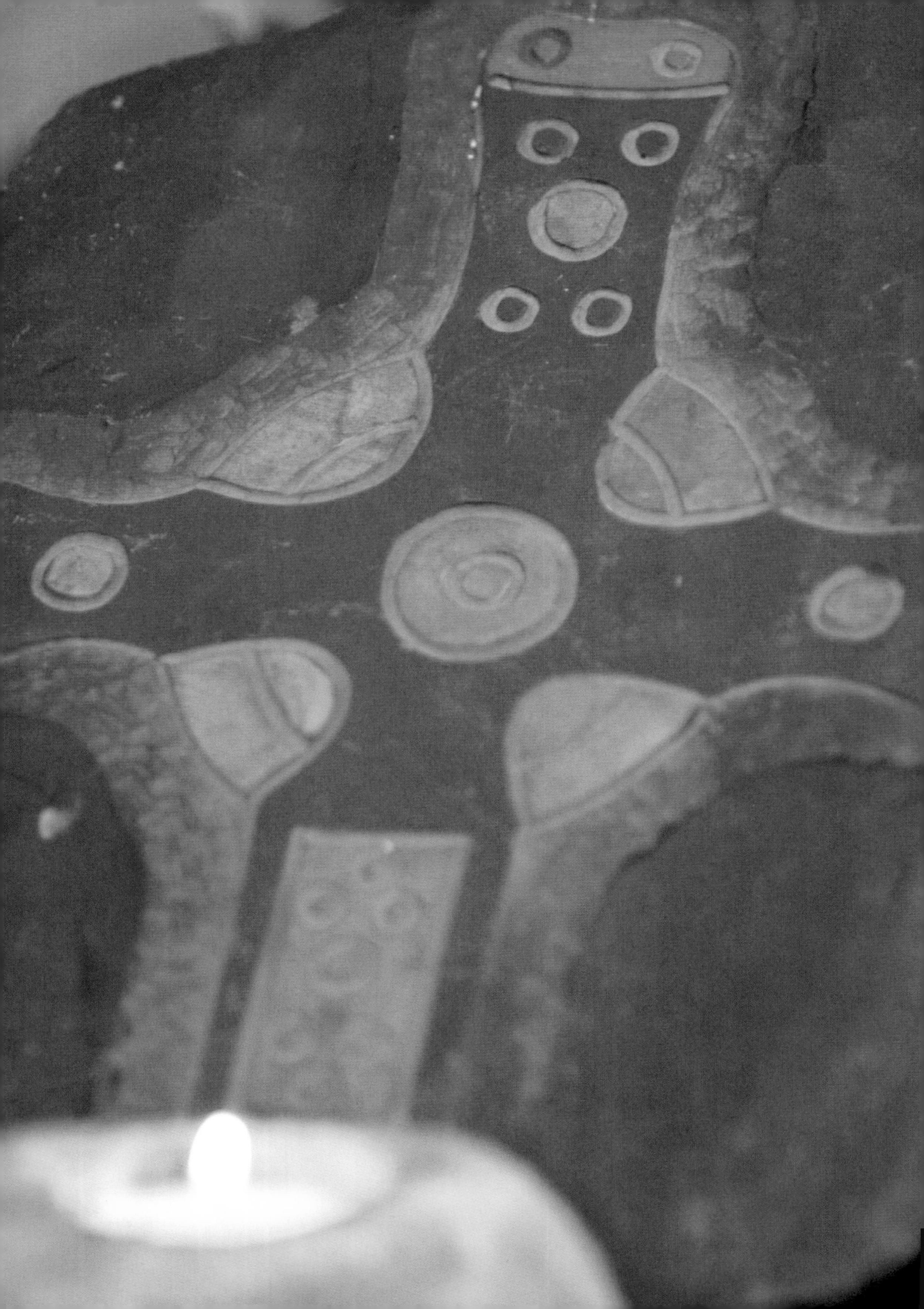

Drama Part 2

In full view of everyone.

Peter: But I tell you we *have* seen him. Don't you believe us?

Thomas: No, I don't. It's just not possible. It's against all the laws of nature.

Peter: But I'm telling you, I saw him. We all did. He appeared in this very room.

Thomas: *(Impatiently.)* Yes, yes, as if by magic. You saw what you wanted to see, Peter, locked away in this room, fearing arrest or a traitor's kiss.

Peter: *(In an exasperated voice.)* But it wasn't just here he came. He appeared to Mary, too, in the garden.

Thomas: I know, Mary told me of the vision in the garden. Look, Peter, Mary was upset, probably tearful, certainly emotional. It was in the half-light of early morning, eyes blurred with tears and, suddenly, this man appears. Of course it was the gardener. She even admits that she didn't recognize him. It was only because he knew her name that she believed it was Jesus …

Mary enters and walks quickly up to Peter and Thomas.

Mary: Excuse me, I can speak for myself! I know what I saw. Of course I was upset, but, as he said my name, I knew immediately who it was. If he had been the gardener, don't you think he would have said so?

Thomas: I'm not saying that any of you are lying, just that you are mistaken. It's all very understandable – it has been a terrible time for all of us. If it helps you get over the shock and bereavement of losing a good friend, you believe what you want to, but don't expect me to go along with it. I am just too tired and upset by the whole thing. I have made enough of a fool of myself and I won't let it happen again. Just be careful, that's all. Don't be too keen to share your fantasy with others who may use it against you.

Peter: What can we say to convince you, Thomas?

Thomas: Nothing you say is going to do that. I need concrete proof, to be able to inspect the scars on his body, to touch and feel for myself. Only then will I believe.

Mary: Well, I know that nobody is going to be convinced by the witness of a woman, but Jesus did give me a specific message – to share the news with you all – and that is just what I am going to do, whatever the cost.

Peter and Mary each light one of the candles. Then, all the characters stand perfectly still (freeze) while the passage from John is read.

Leader: (Reads John 20.26–27.)

Thomas: My Lord and my God.

Leader: Jesus said, 'Have you believed because you have seen me? Blessed are those who have not seen and yet have come to believe.'

Thomas comes into view and lights the central white candle.

Leader: Now and again we see.
In those moments of pure joy come
flashes of understanding – when the penny drops and
we see God.

Just now and again
we need to stand on the mountain top
and absorb the panoramic vista,
strain our eyes to search beyond our narrow vision,
look up, look out, look beyond
to the glory of God revealed in the world.

But we must look down, too.
See, nothing much grows on the mountain top
beneath the pilgrim feet
for it is in the valley, among God's people,
in the joy and sorrow of the earth in which we are set, that growth takes place
and there is transformation.

The leader should then invite those present to enter a period of reflection and offer them an opportunity to come and light a tealight to mark a moment in their lives when they believed or as a sign of a commitment to search for truth. Some quiet music may be played.

Leader: The Lord is with us.
All: Thanks be to God.

Leader: Loving God, it's a big step from doubt to belief. Our doubts are real, valid, sensible. We live in a world of science and technology, where things must be tried, tested and proved beyond doubt before they are given the seal of approval.

Your promises seem unreal, impossible, foolish in the eyes of the world and certainly difficult to understand. It's a tough challenge and, let's face it, a risk. We risk looking foolish, gullible and naive.

So what?! We prove our love by doing loving things. So what if we cannot prove belief, at least let us live as if we believe it.

Lord, we believe, help our unbelief.

Play the Handel piece or other suitable music that you have chosen.

Leader: Loving God, we want to follow you, but we are frightened – frightened that we will have to let go of some of the things we cling to. Frightened that we will have to emerge from places of safety and protection that we have shaped for ourselves, where we feel comfortable and secure, and risk living in your presence. We don't feel confident enough or good enough. Forgive us.
All: Help us to see the way forward.

Leader: Loving God, we want to follow Jesus, but we are frightened – frightened of what people will say. Frightened that we will lose our friends, our status, our integrity. We are frightened that, in saying 'Yes' to you, we will have to say 'No' to some of those things we cherish and revere. Forgive us.
All: Help us to see the way forward.

Leader: Loving God, we want to follow Jesus, to say 'Yes' to the new challenges, but we are frightened. Frightened that we will lose control of our lives, that too much will be asked of us – more than we are prepared to give. We are frightened of failure, looking foolish, being laughed at. We know that, in following Jesus, we too will have to speak up for those on the edges of our society, speak out against injustice, check the racist remark, the unkind word. It won't be easy, but then you never promised that it would be. Forgive us.
All: Help us to see the way forward.

Leader: Loving God, you meet us where we are, with all our fears and anxieties, and walk with us. Hiding away, you come searching for us, gently luring us with words of tenderness and love. Give us courage to say 'Yes' to your call and eyes to see you in all your glory.
All: Amen.

Meditation

Things look different from up here

Based on Luke 19.1–10.
This could be spoken by someone from the top of a stepladder.

You get a different perspective from up here. You can see so much further, for one thing. A larger picture, not just one part of it. You can see things much more clearly. See what's going on and where you are in relation to everyone else. It's a comfortable place in some ways – just viewing from a distance, you don't have to be involved. Most people are so absorbed in getting on with their own lives that they don't look up and see you sitting 10 feet above contradiction.

I used to be like that. I sometimes wondered what happened to people after I had collected the taxes and my commission, of course. Well, we all have to live, don't we? Go along with the system. If you don't, society will collapse and anarchy will reign.

The truth is, I was always a little uncomfortable about it, and working for the Romans made me no friends, I can tell you. So I was really just wanting to see him from my vantage point. Interested to observe.

Then he looked up, called me by my name, invited me to be his friend. I knew then, in that moment, what I had to do. I had to come down from my place of safety and commit myself to change. *(Pause.)*

Life has never been the same since.

chapter four **the healing touch**

‘To enjoy life we must touch much of it lightly.’

– Voltaire

chapter four
the healing touch

From the moment of our birth, there are hands to receive us, hold us and care for us in our vulnerability. At the end of our earthly life, hands prepare us for our final journey, as we are placed back into the hands of God. In between, we use our own hands to explore our environment and relationships and pursue our lives.

Just beneath the skin, we have millions of sensory receptors, which help us to respond immediately to what is happening on the surface of our bodies, whether it is the light touch of a kiss of greeting or cold, heat or pain. For example, if we put our hands into a bowl of very hot water, a message is sent to the spinal cord and on to the brain, which then sends one back to nerves that make us respond by quickly withdrawing our hands from the water.

Some areas of our bodies are more sensitive than others. Our fingertips are extremely sensitive as our hands and fingers are the primary means of exploring our environment.

We talk, too, about being 'touched', not physically but when our emotions are engaged, when we feel moved by someone's act of love, by their sadness or generosity.

Inspired by the Bible

On the fringe (Mark 5)

Some versions of the Bible say that the woman touched the fringe of Jesus' 'garment'. It is possible that the Jewish prayer shawl – the tallith – is meant. In biblical times, all Jewish males would wear the tallith, around the edges of which are knotted fringes. The knots are visible reminders of the number of commandments given in the Old Testament. The word tallith means 'a little tent'. So, as the tallith is drawn over the head during a time of prayer, it becomes a little prayer tent for the wearer, a holy place. To be wrapped in the prayer shawl is symbolic of being wrapped in the mercy, will and love of God. Even today for the Jewish people, the tallith is a religious symbol, a garment, shroud, canopy, a cloak that encircles them, both physically and spiritually, within prayer.

It is thought by some that the apostle Paul, who is described in the New Testament as a tentmaker, could, in fact, have been a maker of talliths.

She had made up her mind. It was worth the risk, worth condemnation, anger, even physical violence. She was desperate enough to try anything. No one else had been able to help, but

Jesus might just be able to. He had done it for others, so why not for her? She felt that he was her last chance.

It was her brother who had told her that Jesus was in the neighbourhood when he had come to leave food for her. He had not come in, of course – just left the offering by the door. Nobody came in now – her condition made sure of that. He had also told her the news that Jairus' daughter was very ill. She remembered little Rachel being born. It was soon afterwards that she had become ill and for 12 years now she had borne the stigma of her illness – the bleeding that meant she was excluded from society as it made her unclean in the eyes of the law and, thus, a danger to everyone else. According to Jewish law, anyone who associated with her, touched her or anything she had touched would be contaminated. She longed to be able to go out, meet with friends and have guests for meals, but, most of all, she wanted some human contact, to feel the warmth of human hands. Her body craved it, like a parched desert craves water.

She had had a little money of her own, but what she had she'd spent on physicians. Then, when that failed, she tried all the remedies suggested in the Talmud, such as drinking tonic made from a compound of rubber alum and garden crocus dissolved in wine, wearing the ash of an ostrich's egg in a linen bag around her neck. It had been difficult to find an ostrich's egg, but worse was having to obtain a barleycorn found in the dung of a white she ass and rub it over herself. Nothing worked. What a waste of time and money it had all been. Now, almost destitute, she had to rely on family to give her handouts from time to time.

This was going to be her last chance. If this failed, life was over. The day was hot, but she wrapped herself in her cloak and pulled it well over her head. She went the back way round the streets, in order to avoid the bustle of the marketplace, and out into the countryside. Her mouth was dry and she felt sick with apprehension. 'Please God,' she prayed, 'don't let anyone recognize me. I know I must not touch this holy man Jesus, but let me reach him, so that I can just touch the fringe of his prayer shawl. That will be enough.'

Suddenly, she could see the crowd. It was larger than she had imagined, but, worse than that, she recognized Jairus, leader of the synagogue, talking to a man she took to be Jesus. If Jairus recognized her, all would be lost. Her home, which had been like a tomb to her for so long, now seemed a place of safety and solace. There was a moment's hesitation as the thought of returning there flashed into her mind, but, no, she had come this far, she wasn't going to turn back now. She put her head down and weaved her way in and out of the crowd until she could see the fringe of Jesus' shawl. One last stretch and she had made it. Almost crumpling in a heap at his feet she suddenly felt elation at the achievement. She had done it, touched his garment, and she felt better just for that. Now she could go home and no one would know.

'Who touched me?' he said – the words drove a stake of fear into her. She didn't move as other voices dismissed the need to know. With so many people clambering to get close, it could have been anyone, they said, and the need to get to Jairus' house was urgent – his child was on the verge of death. The question was repeated: 'Who touched me?' He wasn't going to let it be. It was over. She had been found out. Slowly, she rose to her feet. 'It was me,' she whispered. 'Tell me why?' he said. 'Let us all know why.' The crowd was getting restless and she could feel Jairus' eyes on her. She could sense the unspoken words: 'Why waste time with her? She's been ill for 12 years – another few hours will make no difference, Jesus – get your priorities right!'

Jesus persisted and, for the first time, she had been able to speak about her isolation, her loneliness, her despair. He held out his hand to her then and called her daughter: 'My daughter, your faith has made you well. Go in peace.' As he said those words, there came the news that the child was dead. She was appalled. Had her healing been at the expense of Rachel's life? Jesus, however, appeared unconcerned as he told Jairus not to worry and continued to move towards his house. The crowd followed, leaving her alone.

It was later that she learned Rachel was well again. In fact, a number of people came to tell her the news and celebrate her own release from the bondage of religious prejudice and taboo. She had been received back into the community. For the first time in 12 years she was truly home.

Inspired by a memory

No longer untouchable

Leprosy – or Hansen's disease, to give it its less frightening title, for it was Dr Hansen who, in l873, identified the bacteria that causes leprosy – is a chronic medical condition affecting mainly the nerves, skin, eyes and nose. It attacks nerve endings and, if untreated, eventually loss of feeling occurs in the fingers and toes, which, in turn, in advanced cases, can result in unfelt injuries or leading to deformity. It is thought that leprosy is spread by droplet infection – that is, by coughing and sneezing – but is not highly infectious. It is neither hereditary nor contagious. You cannot become infected by touching someone with leprosy and, in fact, 95 per cent of the world's population is totally immune. It is a disease that, since biblical times, has struck fear into the hearts of humankind. In medieval times in England, a priest would read the burial service over someone with leprosy, pronounce them dead to the world but alive to Christ and then banish them from the community.

I met Mr Patel in November 2001 on a visit to one of the Leprosy Mission Hospitals in South India. He was a tall, dignified man of 60. Some 11 years earlier, he had been admitted to hospital with leprosy. He responded well to treatment and, within two years, he was pronounced cured and ready to return to his own village and the home in which he had lived all his life until his illness. However, that was not to be as his village community forbade him to return. In their ignorance, they felt him still to be a threat. The very word leprosy drove fear into their hearts. He must not return and put the community in danger, they said, so he remained in one of the 'mercy homes' in the hospital grounds.

Most leprosy hospitals have mercy homes where people who have been abandoned by their families and ostracised by communities are allowed to stay. This is less of a problem now because, as well as identifying sufferers and effecting a cure, there is an ongoing campaign to educate people about the disease and the myths that surround it. Indeed, some people from Mr Patel's village had recently been visited and the result was that they now felt confident enough to allow him to come back home.

I arrived on the day he was due to go back to his home for an official visit – the first in 11 years – and was invited to join with him and hospital officials.

We climbed into the Jeep for the drive to the village, just a few miles away. Mr Patel sat upright in the vehicle, with his hands in his lap, The staff talked positively and encouraged him to believe that all would be well, but I could see that he was apprehensive.

We stopped at the edge of the village, stepped out of the Jeep and walked the final few yards. People looked up from their various tasks, saying brief words of welcome, and some put down their tools or picked up their babies and followed us. By the time we had reached Mr Patel's old home, there was quite a crowd. A more formal welcome was made by the village elder and we all shook hands or used the greeting 'Namaste', putting our hands together as if to pray and bowing as we said it.

I sensed that there was still some unease on the part of the village folk and Leprosy Mission staff, as if both were testing out the situation, unsure of how to proceed. I watched Mr Patel as, with tears in his eyes, he looked at the ruins of his old home. For 11 years, no one had lived in it, for fear that it might be contaminated with leprosy, and so it had been left to fall into disrepair. Like the effects of the disease itself, it had wasted away, forgotten, isolated, disregarded. The Leprosy Mission had agreed that it would fund the rebuilding of the two-roomed house, for all that was left were crumbling walls and the lintel and frame of the front door.

Mr Patel walked forwards, stood in the doorway with his hands spread out to touch each side of the doorframe and, with tears streaming down his face, he said, 'I have come home. This is my home.'

Smiles and tears broke out on the faces of the people. The taboo had been broken. After 11 years, he had been reinstated in his rightful place in the community.

Questions for reflection

Who do you feel are the people on the fringes of our society today?
Who are the people we don't want to have living near us?
Who are the people we avoid and isolate in our society?
Who do we not want to touch?
If we were able to touch Jesus, what healing would we be asking for?

Reflective exercise

Hands

Have available a ballpoint pen, a bowl of water that is large enough for you to put both hands in to and move them about, a small hand towel and some lavender or other aromatic hand cream.

Sit in your favourite quiet spot and, either in silence or with some contemplative background music playing, look carefully at your hands for a few minutes.

Consider all the things you do with your hands in the course of a day and how you use them to communicate and interact with those around you.

It may be that your hands are arthritic, or perhaps you have had a stroke, or an accident has left you with the use of one hand only or fingers that are stiff and swollen. Still, look at and consider them carefully. After a few minutes, read Isaiah 49.13–16. Then, open your hands out, palms upwards and read the following.

God, you know us so well,
you have even written our names on the palm of your hand.

Remember the times when you have opened your hands to others, in welcome and in friendship,
when you have used your hands to soothe a child in pain
or comfort a friend in sorrow,
a time when, in silence, you have just held a hand because there were no words to say,
that moment when you have touched the pulse of another's fear or taken the hand of a stranger who was lost and confused.
Think of a time when you have placed your hands in the hands of others,
the moments when you have clapped your hands in sheer joy or blown a kiss from them.
Sometimes it was easy to do, but, with open hands, we are exposed to rejection, we are open and vulnerable.
Sometimes it is easier to keep our hands clasped shut for fear of hurt.

Close hands into tight fists.

Remember the times when you have used your hands destructively,
building barriers that have excluded others,
when you have refused the hand of a stranger,
closed your hands in anger and fear,
pointed a finger of scorn or accusation,
shaken a fist in temper,
thrown or torn something in anger,
refused a helping hand,
rejected an offer of reconciliation and peace.

Now open your hands. See the beauty of them and know that, whatever you may have done or not done, you are held in the hollow of God's hand.

Take a few more moments to think and then take up the pen and write on the palms of your hands the names of people, places or situations that you want to bring before God today. Think of them for a few minutes.

When you are ready, gently lower your hands into the bowl of water, cupping them to allow the water to trickle through your fingers and wash over the names you have written for as long as you like. Read and think about the following as you do so.

God, you inscribe our names on the palms of each of your hands,
wash us in your tenderness and compassion,
refresh and fragrance us with your love
that we may hold before you those who are touched only by
hunger, pain and isolation,
whose lives are dry and arid.
May we carry them in our hands today.

When you feel ready, dry your hands, making sure that you do not erase the names you have written on them. Massage hand cream into them and continue to think about the people whose names are on our palms.

Be conscious today of the things or people you touch. May you touch everything with reverence and care.

Worship material

Good news

Preparation

For this and the following worship ideas included below, the following items and display are suggested, but you may wish to adapt them to suit your circumstances:

- a recording of a peal of bells, a set of handbells or one bell
- a jug containing olive oil to which some drops of sandalwood essential oil have been added (obtainable from chemists) and a number of small dishes into which some of the scented oil has been decanted
- a length of wool or string for each person – at least 50 cm long
- pieces of sacking (hessian).

For the display, lay a bright red cloth on a small table and place on it a number of pebbles and stones of various sizes and colours around one large central candle. If possible, include a piece of sandalwood or other wood of a reasonable size and one or two twigs from a thorny bush, such as pyracantha or holly. Arrange a broken pot, such as a small terracotta plantpot, next to these.

Lay a tallith (Jewish prayer shawl) on the display. If you are unable to obtain one, a piece of material with a fringe will do.

Arrange for the people attending to sit in two circles. If this is not possible and they are in rows, place them so that the first and every alternate row after that can turn to face the row behind.

You will need three people to be the 'voices' in the piece. They should be dispersed around the church or meeting place and their lines shouted out.

A peal of bells – either handbells or a recording of them – could be used. If this is not possible, there should be at least one bell that is rung between the sentences delivered by the voices.

Finish the first piece below with a hymn or reflective piece of music, such as 'God's Spirit is in my heart', *Hymns & Psalms* 315 and other sources based on Isaiah 61.1–4.

The event

Voice 1: Good news!

Voice 2: Good news!

Voice 3: Good news!

Voices 1, 2 and 3:
Good news!

Ringing of bells or single bell.

Voice 1: The Spirit of the Lord is upon me.

Voice 2: He has chosen me to bring good news to the poor.

Voice 3: To those who live in desperate poverty, those who scratch a meagre living from poor soil, families who have lost their homes and possessions, those who have been denied meaningful relationships.

Ring bell or bells.

Voice 1: The Spirit of the Lord is upon me.

Voice 2: He has sent me to proclaim liberty to the captives.

Voice 3: To those who are slaves to poverty due to the greed of others, those who are enslaved by addictions, those who are imprisoned in their own fears and prejudices, those who have been incarcerated by oppressive regimes.

Ring bell or bells.

Voice 1: The Spirit of the Lord is upon me.

Voice 2: He has sent me to give sight to the blind.

Voice 3: To those who can see no way to turn, those blind to another point of view, those sightless to the suffering of others.

Ring bell or bells.

Voice 1: The Spirit of the Lord is upon me.

Voice 2: He has sent me to set the oppressed free.

Voice 3: To those broken by life's experiences, those exploited by unfair trading, those demoralized by unemployment, those denied education.

Ring bell or bells.

Voices 1, 2 and 3 together:
We have come to announce that the time has come when the Lord will save his people. Good news, good news!

Ring bell or bells. Finish with chosen hymn or piece of music.

Warning bells

Preparation

This drama could be played out with the whole congregation or, alternatively, two people or groups of two could play it out for all to see. They should face each other and be an arm's length apart. Two other people could read as the groups act out the words. The minimum number of people needed is three – the leader and two actors.

Have a bell or bells that can be rung when indicated below or a recording of them that can be played. At the end, during the sharing of the peace, the congregation could sing 'The peace of the Lord' by Brian Hoare (*Big Blue Planet*) or another peal of bells could be played.

The event

Leader: In New Testament times, those suffering from leprosy and other contagious diseases would be required to shout a warning of their approach. In the Middle Ages, this might have been accompanied by the ringing of a bell. Throughout history, bells have been used to warn of danger and invasion, but also as a means of gathering people together for celebration and prayer.

Ring bell.

No. 1: (With arms and hands extended, like a policeman stopping traffic.)
No – go away, go away, don't come near. *(Turn around.)*

No. 2: (With arms extended, hands palms uppermost.)
You remember us. You have seen us on your television screens. Victims of drought and famine, some of us are HIV positive, some have AIDS, hepatitis, cholera and TB. We thought you cared. Have pity, have pity.

No. 1: (Turning around, with both arms extended making pushing away movements without touching the other person. Ring bell.)

Don't come any closer.

We can cope with you at a distance, in the comfort and security of our homes, through the camera lens and the satellite link.

We can shed our tears for you, reach in our pockets for you, but we cannot face you, hold out our hands to you. We don't want you near us. We are so afraid. Go away, go away, go away.

No. 2: (Arms at side, ring bell.)

Then who will help us? Who will show us they care? Who will touch us? Who will say 'yes'?

Bible reading: Mark 1.40-45.

Leader: This is the word of God.
All: Yes, yes, yes.

Sharing of the peace.

Leader: May the peace of the Lord be always with you.
All: And also with you.

People share the peace with one another and sing or listen to the bells, as you have decided.

To feel or not to feel – meditation

Look at your hands and feet and imagine for a moment that you have no sense of feeling in them. Just imagine not being able to feel:

- the delicacy of a flower or the sharpness of a thorn
- the hardness of stone or the fragility of an egg
- water running through your fingers or sand trickling between your toes
- rich brown earth crumbling at your touch or squishy mud under your feet
- the silky soft fur of a much-loved pet
- a wriggling worm
- the numbing chill of a snowball in the hand
- the roughness of coarse-woven wool or the smooth slipperiness of silks and satins
- being wrapped in a large soft towel after a bath
- cool tiles beneath your feet on a hot summer's day
- comforting hot water bottles on a cold winter's night
- light downy duvets or cool cotton sheets.

Think about the best feelings of all:

- the touch of love, to hold and cherish in the act of love
- holding a newborn baby
- the clasp of the hand of a friend
- the touch of God, felt in all the good things of life, the abundance of creation and the knowledge of God's love.

'I will not forget you. I have written your name on the palms of my hands' (Isaiah 49.16, adapted).

Prayers

Preparation

Distribute the small dishes of oil around the church or room where people can easily get to them or else simply pass them around.

Play a piece of quiet, repetitive music during this activity, such as 'O Lord, hear my prayer', *Laudate*, from the music of Taizé, or 'Celebration' from *Standing Stone* by Paul McCartney.

The event

Suggest that people consider the name they use when they address God and, having dipped a finger into the oil, write that name on the palm of their left hand and then write their own name on their other palm.

Then, ask them to put both hands together, in an attitude of prayer. In doing this we can feel held by God and also that we are holding on to God.

Encourage people, while holding their hands together like this, to pray their own prayers silently.

Reflective exercise

The touching collection

Preparation

This exercise can be done individually or in small groups. For larger gatherings, there would need to be several 'collections'.

Lay out a circle of white cloth or paper and, around it, display a variety of items for people to touch. Include, if possible, things from the following list, but more can be added:

- cotton wool
- a piece of leather
- rough material, such as tweed
- a ball of wool
- a piece of rough wood
- a smooth wood carving

- a dish of earth
- a lump of clay
- a dish of jelly
- a daisy or other small flower
- a stone
- a feather
- a soft toy
- a silk scarf
- a book
- a shoe.

The event

Invite people to sit around the circle, look at the selection of items displayed and think about which item they are most drawn to pick up.

Are there any items they don't want to touch? Are there any that have particular meaning or association for them?

Go round the group, inviting people in turn to choose one item to pick up.

If a number of people want to hold the same object, they should hold up their hands to indicate this and then form their own group with the item being passed round.

Think silently about what you feel as you touch and explore it with your hands. Is there a story to tell associated with the item?

Invite those who would like to do so to share their thoughts, even if it is only a word.

Knotting prayers

The event

Older people in the congregation will probably remember being told as children to tie a knot in their handkerchief when they wanted to remember something (not so easy with paper tissues!).

Invite people to tie a knot in their piece of wool or string to remember a person, situation, country or issue, thinking prayerfully about it as they do so. This should be done in silence or with some quiet music playing in the background.

If desired, people can share one of their 'knots' with a neighbour.

Afterwards, they can either be collected and brought forward to lay on the altar or Communion table with the offertory or each person can tie the ends of their prayer string together and it can be worn as a necklace or put in a pocket and taken home. This can later be used as a 'rosary' to prompt prayers or action during the week.

At the end of the prayers of intercession, use the following blessing.

Leader: (This blessing was used while wrapping oneself in the tallith.)
Blessed art thou, Lord God King of the Universe, who has made us holy with his commandments and who has commanded us to wrap ourselves in the fringes.

Our sackcloth

Preparation

Give each member of the group or congregation a small piece of sacking (hessian) to hold. Sackcloth was often worn during Lent in medieval times by people who felt a need to show how sorry they were for wrongs they had done. The roughness of the cloth next to their skin was a constant reminder of their sins. Most of us don't need such an uncomfortable prompt – we are only too well aware of our own shortcomings!

You may wish to play background music during the part towards the end when people are asked to reflect on a series of questions. John Williams' 'Hymn to the Fallen', from *Saving Private Ryan*, or John Rutter's 'The Lord is my Shepherd' are both suitable choices.

The event

Leader: Loving and understanding God, we are not really bad people – tempted to do terrible things such as murder, robbery, embezzlement or fraud. We are not tempted to perform terrorist acts or con old people out of their life savings or abuse or threaten violence to others.

Who knows what we are capable of when we are put to the test? Under extreme provocation, might we not all be capable of murder? If our children were starving, would we not be tempted to steal? We might like to think that, even in the most severe of circumstances, we would be able to resist doing the wrong thing, but who knows?

God, who understands the deepest thoughts of our hearts, stand with us and protect us when circumstances threaten to break us and we are tempted to do wrong.

All: Amen

Leader: Loving and understanding God, we are not really bad people, tempted by 'big' sins, but we are often tempted to be lazy about doing good things. There are times when we say, 'I really cannot be bothered', 'It's not my concern', times when apathy takes over or we go along with the rest of the crowd for a quiet life, even when we know we should take a different viewpoint.

Loving God, who understands what it's like to be tempted, stand with us and protect us from apathy, lack of compassion, prejudice and ignorance, settling for cheap, simplistic answers and an easy life.

All: Amen

Invite people to reflect on the following questions while holding the piece of sacking. Play the music you have chosen.

Leader: What feels rough and uncomfortable in your life? What are the wilderness places for you? What are the problems you wrestle with? What things in your life do you regret? Can anything be done about them?

Recall the names of people who stand by you in times of difficult choices and give thanks to God for them.

People could be invited to take home their sacking, to feel and reflect on during the period of Lent.

Leader: 'You have touched us and turned our mourning into dancing
Removed our sackcloth and clothed us with joy.
We cannot be silent in your presence
But will give you thanks and praise for ever' (Psalm 30.11, adapted).

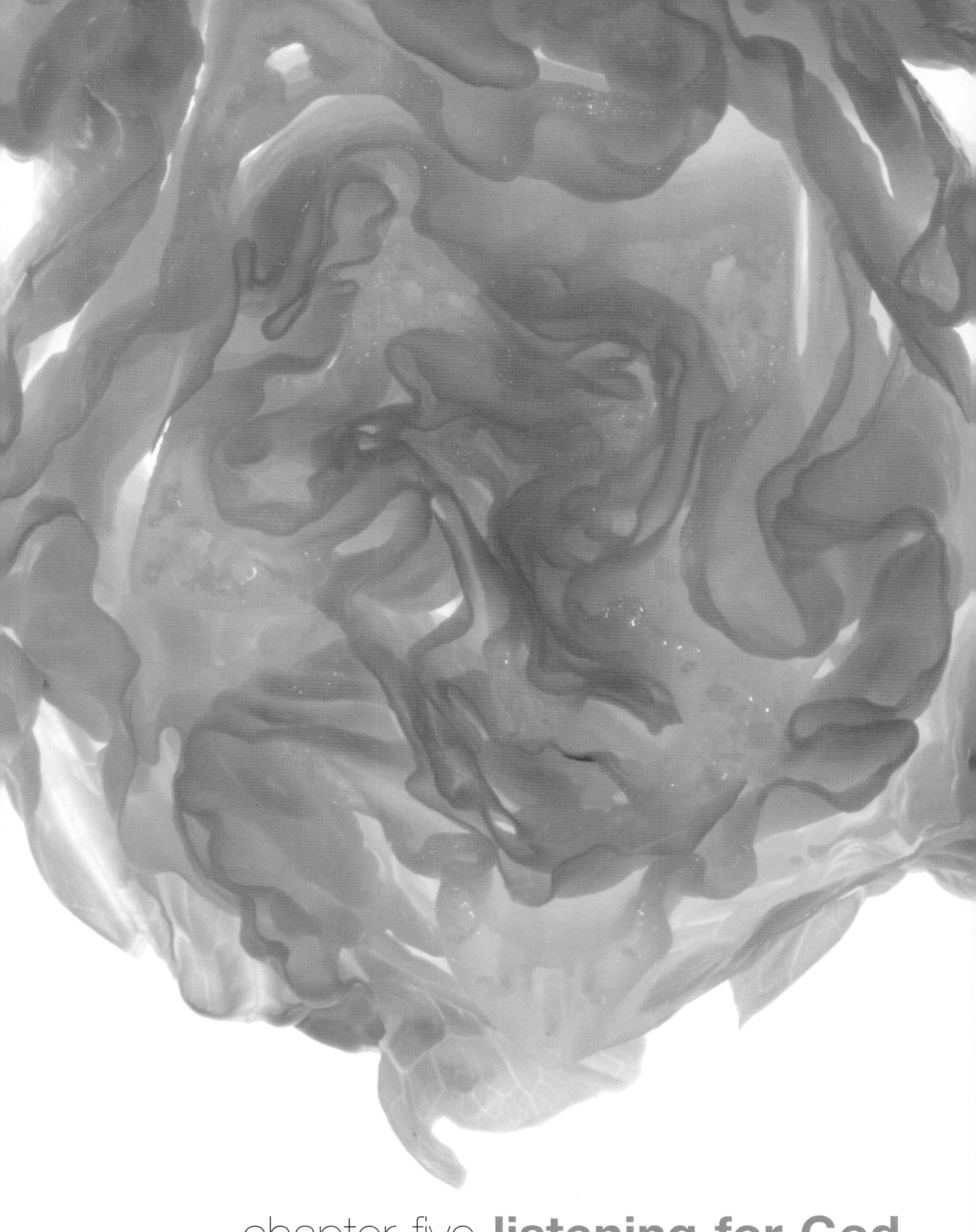

chapter five **listening for God**

'Hearing is a form of touch.
You feel it through your body and sometimes
it almost hits your face.'

– Evelyn Glennie

chapter five
listing for God

Sounds are vibrations, which undertake an amazing journey, passing from the outer ear and being funnelled along to the ear canal until they hit the eardrum, causing it to vibrate. This causes the ossicles – the three smallest bones in the body – to start moving, causing wave-like motions in the fluid inside the cochlea, the snail-shaped organ of hearing. The journey continues as the sensory hair cells in the cochlea are stimulated, which in turn send nerve impulses to the brain, which interprets the sounds we hear. Although we can manage enough with just one ear, sound reaches our two ears at different times, allowing us to locate the direction of the sound.

Hearing is the one sense that is active even when we are asleep. It stays alert to protect us from possible night-time dangers, hence the need for a smoke alarm as the smell of smoke would not necessarily wake us.

We live in a world in which thousands of different languages are spoken. We might be able to hear them, but not necessarily understand what is being said. Even with our mother tongue we sometimes misunderstand or choose to turn a 'deaf ear' to what someone is saying.

Inspired by the Bible

A midday conversation (John 4)

She eyed the empty water jar in the corner of the room and sighed deeply. It was time for her lonely journey.

The other women had returned hours ago, laughing and chattering together. Drops of precious water splashed from their brim-filled containers as they shifted the weight on their shoulders, turned to laugh at some joke or bent their heads in conspiratorial whispered gossip. Later, in the cool of the evening, the ritual would be repeated and she would hear them once again returning wearily to their homes and families.

The trips to the well were special times for the women – a time for sharing those things that women like to share without the constraints of husband or children. It was heavy work, though, for the well – Jacob's well – was nearly a mile away. It wasn't too bad going, but returning with the jars full of water was a killer, especially the evening trip after a tiring day's work. Still, they were used to it. It was women's work, the men said, but not many of them had carried a heavy jar of water twice a day a mile and back. No, men had more important things to do. The well was the women's space and, for them, it was a sacred place.

She missed out on that social interaction, the chat, the company, the gossip and secrets shared – they had made it clear right from the start that they did not want her around. Nothing was said, at first, but she noticed that they turned away when she approached and lowered their voices, pushing in front of her in the queue and eyeing her with contempt. She had tried to be friendly, but they had ignored her. She was excluded from their company and pushed to the margins of acceptable society.

The final straw had come when one of the women had pushed into her, muttering something about contaminating the well. She had dropped her jar and it had smashed, leaving her with neither water nor container. In sheer misery she slumped by the well, covered her head and cried. They had left her then and, when her tears were finished, she had slowly walked back home, empty-handed. He had shouted at her, called her harsh names and made her return with another container to fill. Since then, she had made the journey for water when she knew that people would be resting from the heat of the noonday sun.

She hoisted the empty jar up on to her shoulder, slipped out into the blistering heat and began the long journey to the well, reflecting, for the hundredth time as she walked along the hot and rough road, on how she had come to this point.

It wasn't all her own fault, surely, but still she felt the weight of her circumstances, as heavy as the physical burden she was carrying. She knew that the other women saw her as a threat, with her slim figure, unchanged by pregnancy (another guilt she had to carry), her glorious unruly hair peeping out from under her head covering, her smooth skin and deep dark eyes. Five times married, true, but death and divorce had made others suspicious of her. Without family support and the status that came with having children, she was destitute, so when Josh came along, offering to give her a roof over her head and food in her belly in exchange for services she might render, she had grasped the opportunity with both hands. He wasn't a bad man, really, or unkind, but he didn't want marriage and, as she was unlikely to bear him a son, why bother? She was a survivor and surviving the only way left open to her.

Approaching the well, she stopped suddenly. To her distress, she saw a man with his back to her sitting by the well. Her immediate thought was to turn and run, knowing how it would be interpreted. Who would believe that she had not planned a secret assignation? In the moment that she was thinking about this, he turned to face her. She noticed that he was a Jew.

'Will you give me a drink, please?' he asked. Why was he speaking to her? Jews did not speak to Samaritans and certainly not to female ones. She covered her face and lowered her eyes before responding. 'How is it that you ask me for a drink?'

'Ah,' he replied, 'if you knew the gift God is offering you and who it is that is asking you for water, you would ask *me* for a drink and I would give you living water.'

He is teasing me, she thought. Well, two could play that game. 'You have no bucket, sir, and the well is deep, so where do you get that living water? Are you greater than our ancestor Jacob, who gave us the well and, with his sons and his flocks, drank from it?'

She busied herself drawing up the water, as he replied, 'Everyone who drinks of this water will be thirsty again, but those who drink of the water that I will give them will never be thirsty. The water that I will give will become in them a spring of water gushing up to eternal life.'

She was starting to get annoyed by this nonsense. Was he trying it on with her or setting a trap to catch her out? She swung the bucket up on to the rim of the well, water splashing out of it as she banged it down. 'Well, give me this water – I would like not to be thirsty again or have to make this journey to the well every day,' she said, and she meant it.

'Go, then, and call your husband.' The words, thrust into her like a knife. Oh, good God, no! It *was* a trap after all. Did even this stranger know about her life?

'I have no husband,' she said quietly, waiting for the words of condemnation to be spat out and for people to appear, perhaps with stones, to chase her away. They held each other's gaze for some moments. She couldn't remember when anyone had ever looked at her like that. Then he said gently, 'What you have said is true', but that was all. It was as if he just wanted to establish the facts about her.

Who was this man, so unlike any other man she had ever met? Intuitively she knew that he was different, important.

'You must be a prophet,' she said, and meant it. It was then, for the next few minutes, they conversed about the long-standing dispute between Jew and Samaritan over the correct place to worship God. 'People must worship God in spirit and in truth,' he had explained, 'the place is not important.' 'Well, I know that the Messiah is coming and, when he does, he will explain all things to us,' she responded.

'I am the one,' he said.

She was still taking in the implications of this when other men appeared. They stood a little way back, clearly scandalized by the picture in front of them. She smiled at their embarrassment. She took her opportunity to leave and suddenly realized that she needed to tell someone about the encounter.

She was no longer afraid. This man had treated her with respect, giving her back her dignity as a human being. He had released something within her and she had a great desire to tell everyone what he had done for her.

It was not until later that evening, after she had persuaded the whole village to 'come and see the man Jesus – the man who told me', that she realized she had left her water jar behind. Indeed, she had left more than that.

Inspired by a memory

The sound of music

One of my earliest memories is of my mother singing to me, mostly Scottish lullabies and love songs. My father, a Welshman, loved male voice choirs and his brother, David Jones, was the principal tenor in the one at the local colliery. He was known as Dai Jones Top Note, to distinguish him from all the other David Joneses in the valley.

At the age of 14, I bought a wind-up record player from a church jumble sale. It came with a small tin box of needles and two records. One was Mario Lanza singing 'Drink, drink, drink' from *The Student Prince*. The other was the overture to Smetana's *Bartered Bride*. I was much impressed by the latter piece, although for a long time I thought it was called the 'battered' bride. However, it was at the age of 16, when Alan took me to Covent Garden to hear a performance of Mozart's *The Marriage of Figaro,* that I really fell in love with classical music.

I can remember it so clearly, viewing from up in the gods the magnificent setting of the building itself, the evening dresses – that was in the days when people dressed up to go to the opera – the sparkling lights, the sense of excitement. Then, that moment of hushed anticipation when the conductor raised the baton and the orchestra began to play the overture. It was as though the music vibrated through the whole of my body. It was stunning, a moment that simply took my breath away, an indescribable feeling of joy. Even now, when I hear that piece of music, it transports me back to that day.

Inner sounds – a reflective exercise

If you have a large conch shell – the sort you used to put to your ear as a child to listen to the sea – put that on the table, together with a tray of sand and a small shell.

If you have a copy of A.A. Milne's *The House at Pooh Corner*, you might like to read for yourself the story of how Pooh, Rabbit and Piglet get lost in a sandpit. The trio find themselves going round and round in circles in the mist, until Pooh announces that, although he doesn't know the way, he has 12 pots of honey in the cupboard at home calling to him and, if no one speaks and he can just listen to the pots, he will know which way home is.

Sometimes it feels as though we are going round and round in circles in our lives, from one thing to another and back again, unable to step off the treadmill of our busyness.

For a moment, sit with your thumbs over your ears and your fingers over your eyes and just listen to your inner self. What can you hear? How do you feel? Cut off? Alone? Peaceful? Uncomfortable?

After a few minutes, lower your hands to your lap and consider the following questions:

- What voices and noises intrude on your life? Are there people always clamouring for your attention?
- Who do you go to for advice? Whose voice do you listen to?

- How do you interpret what you hear?
- How and where do you search for the voice of God?
- Whose voice do you try to ignore?
- Is there anyone you need to listen to today?

If you have a conch shell, put it to your ear and listen for the sea.

Place the small shell in the centre of the tray of sand. This represents you. The shell once housed a sea creature. The shell protected it from harm. The shell provided its defence.

Are there things that you feel you would like to hide away from? Where do you go when things get tough? What acts as your 'shell'?

Write the names of those who are giving you a difficult time at the moment in the sand with your finger. Alternatively, write a word to describe a situation that you are having to deal with.

Think about each one for a moment, bringing them into your mind before God. Then, gently rub your hand over the name or words so that they are no longer visible.

Worship material

Christmas voices – an interactive act of worship

Preparation

Lay a large, circular piece of green cloth on the floor or over a low table. Around the edge, place five large red candles (in suitable containers) with a cluster of small tealights around each one. In the centre, place a larger white candle. Scatter in between evergreen, red berries, oranges, cinnamon sticks, small red apples, fir cones and so on.

Around this, have the leader and characters sitting on cushions or low chairs and the others (the congregation or audience) sitting on chairs in an outer circle, leaving a little space between the two circles.

Apart from the leader, you will need to have 10 people to play the characters.

The characters are teamed up in twos and so should sit close to each other, with space between each pair of characters, who are:

- Zechariah and Joseph
- Mary and Elizabeth
- Herod and a wise man
- A shepherd and the innkeeper
- Simeon and Anna.

If desired, the characters could be in costume.

Organize some music to play at the beginning, such as J.S. Bach's 'Opening Chorus' from the *Christmas Oratorio*, or 'Alle Jahre Wieder' from *Christmas Goes Baroque*. Also, choose music to play after each pair of characters has completed their dialogue, such as Scheidt's 'Puer natus in Bethlehem' for Zechariah and Joseph, 'Magnificat' from *Fountains of Life* by Margaret Rizza for Mary and Elizabeth, Corelli's *Christmas Concerto* (op. 6, no. 8) for Herod and a wise man, Berlioz's *The Childhood of Christ* and 'The Shepherd's Farewell' for a shepherd and the innkeeper, Burgon's 'Nunc dimittis' for Simeon and Anna. To close, you could play the 'Final Chorus' from Bach's *Christmas Oratorio.*

The service could be extended by including readings, dance and carols. The music suggestions made above are just that – feel free to choose your own to suit your situation.

The event

Play the music chosen to begin the event.

Leader: Dear friends, many people have done their best to write a report about the things that have taken place. They wrote what they were told by those who saw these things from the beginning and who broadcast the message. Today, we let those who were there tell you their own stories.

Zechariah and Joseph both stand or turn to face the congregation.

Zechariah: I am an old man.

Joseph: I am a young man.

Zechariah: I had given up hope of becoming a father.

Joseph: I had hopes of becoming a father later.

Zechariah: I was delighted by the news.

Joseph: I was devastated by the news.

Zechariah: I refused to believe it at first. I have to admit, I was struggling to keep awake during my Temple duty that day. The sweet smell of the incense had sent me into a dreamlike state. It was a terrible shock to be confronted with such news -- I just didn't believe it. I was literally speechless. I tried later to explain to Elizabeth using sign language that she was going to have a baby. She thought me raving mad.

Joseph: I *was:* raving mad when Mary told *me:* the news! I was so angry that I shouted at her and called her all sorts of names. Do you know what it feels like to have the one you love tell you that she's going to have a baby and you're not the father?

Zechariah: No, my friend, I do not, but I do know what it feels like to know that other people think that your wife has been unfaithful. Our news brought its own measure of gossip, sly looks and laughter.

Joseph: (Lighting one of the large red candles.)
We light this candle to remember all those who will learn today of the expected birth of a baby.

Zechariah: For those who will delight in the news.

Joseph: For those who will not welcome the news.

Zechariah: For those who cannot wait to tell.

Joseph: For those who don't know who or how to tell.

Zechariah: For those who feel that this child will bring fulfilment and will be waited and prepared for in joy.

Joseph: For those who do not know who the father is and feel alone and isolated.

Zechariah: For those who delight in the prospect of parenthood.

Joseph: (Turns to congregation.)
Are there other people you would like to name? Please come and light one of the small candles for them.

Play some music as people reflect on their prayers.

Mary and Elizabeth stand or turn to face congregation.

Elizabeth: I am an old woman.

Mary: I am a young woman.

Elizabeth: For years I *longed* for a child.

Mary: I longed for a child, but not quite so soon.

Elizabeth: I was past the age to have a child.

Mary: At least you were married – I had to tell my fiancé, Joseph, and my parents that I was pregnant. I risked disgrace and even death. Who would believe that I had not been unfaithful?

Elizabeth: For years I had to bear the disgrace of not being able to conceive, as if somehow it was my fault. Children are regarded as a blessing. We were not blessed in that way. When I first discovered I was pregnant, I hid away for five months.

Mary: I was sent away for three months. It was good to be able to stay with you during that difficult time, though, Elizabeth – to share our experiences, to talk together about our special babies.

Elizabeth: It was a great blessing for me, too, Mary. With Zechariah unable to speak and Joseph far away, we seemed to find our voices, didn't we?

Mary: Do you remember how we danced and sang together? My soul magnifies the Lord and my spirit rejoices in God my Saviour, for he has looked with favour on the lowliness of his servant. Surely from now all generations will call me blessed.

Elizabeth: (Lighting a red candle.)
So we light this candle to remember all those who long for a child.

Mary: For couples going through fertility treatment.

Elizabeth: For those who have suffered the pain of miscarriage and stillbirth.

Mary: For those who have accepted childlessness.

Elizabeth: (To the congregation.)
Are there any other people we should remember? Please come and light a candle for them.

Play some music while people reflect on their prayers. The Magnificat dance later in this chapter could be included here or Mary and Elizabeth could dance as they wish.

Herod and a wise man stand back to back.

Wise man: I am a king.

Herod: I am also a king.

Wise man: I was seeking.

Herod: I was looking.

Wise man: I was tricked.

Herod: I was frightened.

Both turn to face each other.

Wise man: When I came with my companions to the palace looking for this new king, you led us to believe that you wanted to welcome him, too. You asked us to find him and then come and tell you. What we didn't know was that you wanted him out of the way.

Herod: He was a threat! Do you know what it's like always having to keep looking over your shoulder because there is someone ready to stab you in the back and claim the throne for themselves? I was not a popular king, too many enemies.

Wise man: You were ruthless. How *could* you have ordered the deaths of all those innocent babies and made us part of that treachery?

Herod: You were so naive. Anyway, you *didn't* come back, so I had to take other measures. I blame you for that.

Wise man: (Lighting a red candle.)
We light this candle to remember refugees.

Herod: Those who make wrong choices and have to live with the consequences.

Wise man: All those who have to leave their homes and seek safety in another land.

Herod: Those who seek only their own good regardless of what that means for others.

Wise man: (To the congregation.)
Are there any others we should remember? Please come and light a candle for them if you wish.

Play some music while people reflect on their prayers.

The shepherd and innkeeper stand or turn to face the congregation.

Shepherd: I am a humble shepherd.

Innkeeper: I am a humble innkeeper.

Shepherd: I was busy watching the sheep.

Innkeeper: I was busy seeing to all my customers.

Shepherd: I was surprised by a light in the sky and strange music.

Innkeeper: I was surprised by a baby.

Shepherd: I'm used to lambs being born, but living out in the fields day in and day out means that we shepherds are not able to observe all the rituals that our faith requires. People consider us dirty and unclean and we're not supposed to venture into the towns in case we contaminate others, but we felt compelled to take the risk. This was something we had to see for ourselves.

Innkeeper: I am definitely not used to babies being born in my inn! Well, to be truthful, this one wasn't. There was no room, but I am not one to turn customers away and the father was willing to pay for the use of the stable. At least they were out of the way there.

Shepherd: Strange, that. We shepherds are kept out of the way of decent society. We risked losing our jobs, too, leaving the sheep just to come and see a baby. I don't know why we were chosen and, to be honest, I don't really know what it was all about, but I'm glad I came.

Innkeeper: (Lighting a red candle.)
We light this candle to remember all those who work unsociable hours.

Shepherd: Those who open their doors in hospitality.

Innkeeper: Those who sleep on the streets in our cities.

Shepherds: Those regarded as undesirable in our society.

Innkeeper: (To the congregation.)
Are there any others we should remember? Please come and light a candle for them if you wish.

Play some music while people reflect on their prayers.

Simeon and Anna stand or turn to face the congregation.

Simeon: I am an old man.

Anna: I am an old woman.

Simeon: I had waited a long time for this child to be born.

Anna: I have been waiting ever since my husband died over 80 years ago.

Simeon: When I awoke that morning, I knew I had to go to the Temple. It was such a very special moment, when Joseph and Mary came in with the infant Jesus – a fulfilment of all I had been hoping for. I felt I could die in peace after seeing and blessing that baby.

Anna: I just wanted to dance and sing for joy and, although my old bones wouldn't let me, I still had a song in my heart.

Simeon: All our longing and waiting was rewarded.

Anna: (Lighting a red candle.)
We light this candle to remember all those who look for signs of God in the world.

Simeon: For the many older people who, in their wisdom, keep faith with the Church and encourage potential in youngsters.

Anna: Grandparents and godparents and all who give extra support to families.

Simeon: All those who have time to reflect on and contemplate the coming of Jesus.

Anna: Are there any others we should remember? Please light a candle for them if you wish.

After a few moments of silence, play some music while people reflect on their prayers.

Leader: In the beginning was the Word, and the Word was with God, and the Word was God. He was in the beginning with God. All things came into being through him, and without him not one thing came into being. What has come into being in him was life, and the life was the light of all people.

(The centre candle is lit.)
The light shines in the darkness and the darkness did not overcome it.

Close the service with some more music.

The silence of Joseph

How did you feel, Joseph,
when you first heard that Mary was pregnant?
Shocked?
Stunned?
Ashamed?
Sad?
Betrayed?
Guilty?
Were you angry, Joseph?
Did you shout at Mary?
Did you ask why?
Did you call her names, rant and rave?
Did you want to wash your hands of the whole sorry mess?
Walk away, never see her again?

We have never heard your words, Joseph –
not really, except that you were going to finish with her

even if for the best of motives, as you saw it.
Was it *your* suggestion that she go and stay with Elizabeth until it all quietened down?

Did people point the finger at you, Joseph?
Call you names?
'Dirty old man!'
'He couldn't wait!'
Did you feel shamed?
Humiliated?
Guilty?
Did they condemn you?
Say you should have known better?
Did they give you a knowing wink,
as though it was the order of the day,
that it happened all the time,
that it was the woman's responsibility?

But you were prepared to listen to the voice of reason.
You were prepared to risk ridicule and scorn
to do the right thing.
You listened
to Mary and to God's messenger
and so God came to you, in the arms of a woman.

God's song

Melodious God,
the song of creation is yours,
vibrant in tone, diverse in harmony,
perfect in pitch and wide in range.
You are the song, we the singers.

We pray for discernment to interpret this song
when the world sounds flat or out of tune,
for courage to sing out boldly and in unison,
to drown the ugly discordant notes of racism,
injustice, poverty and war.

We pray for compassion to listen to the songs
of the poor and oppressed and to the lament
of those who are too heartbroken to sing.

Give us humility not to crave the solo parts,
but to rejoice in the music of others.

Most of all, we seek the rhythm of your eternal love,
an incarnational song that can be heard as a baby's lullaby.

Magnificat dance

The music for this is 'Magnificat' from *Fountains of Life* by Margaret Rizza.

It is a very slow, meditative dance performed in a circle and starts as the singing begins. It works with any number of dancers and how many you have will depend on how much room you have available, but it is best to have six or more people taking part.

If possible, have different shades of blue scarves tied to the dancers' wrists or little fingers.

1. The dancers stand in a circle, facing in to the centre of it, with their hands held at their sides.
2. Step forward with the right leg, bring the left foot forward to touch the right heel, then place it on the floor. Rise up on to the balls of both feet, then lower feet and step forward with the left leg and bring the right foot forward to touch the heel of the left foot and rise up on to the balls of both feet again. At the same time, raise both arms above shoulder level and clasp the hands of those on either side, forming a 'W' shape.
3. Repeat step 2, but in reverse, starting with the right leg and still holding hands – the arms will now be stretched out sideways. Lean back slightly.
4. Still leaning back, sway to the right, then the left and repeat.
5. Turn to face the right side, still holding hands, and take four steps round in the circle.
6. Drop each other's hands and, individually, turn round in a circle, taking four steps, with hands held high and make slow waving movements with the scarves.

Repeat to the end of the music.

Ears to hear – prayers of intercession

Preparation

Divide the congregation into two groups. Invite them to stand and face each other and cover their ears with their hands. As the sides speak to each other, they cover and uncover their ears as indicated.

Information should be inserted below where marked 'Voice' from up-to-date topical magazines, such as *New Internationalist*, and Christian Aid, Oxfam and other relevant websites.

The event

Leader: (Covering ears.)

How often have we covered our ears, not wanting to hear? Fearful of what speaking out might mean? We speak now of those whose voices you need to hear. Listen to the voices … *(Uncovers ears.)*

Side 1: … of those who suffer violence in their own homes, of children abused by people in whom they placed their trust, of those subjected to racial attacks.

Voice: (Insert current information and/or story.)

Side 2: (Covering ears.)
Stop, we don't want to hear any more. It's not our concern what people do in their own homes. You can't always believe what children say. It's six of one and half a dozen of the other.

Leader: We speak of those whose voices you need to hear. Listen to the voices … *(side 2 uncover their ears.)*

Side 2: … of the hungry in famine-stricken lands, of those who have lost loved ones, livelihoods, everything in floods, droughts and earthquakes, of those oppressed by cruel regimes and corrupt government.

Voice: (Insert current information and/or story.)

Side 1: (Covering ears.)
Stop, we don't want to hear any more. It's not our fault that people live in such places. We give our money when appeals come round. We shouldn't interfere in the politics of another country.

Leader: We speak of those whose voices you need to hear. Listen to the voices … *(Side 1 uncover their ears.)*

Side 1: … of the sad and lonely, of the bereaved and those in pain, of those whose relationships are in a mess, of those with no work, no home, no family.

Voice: (Insert current information and/or story.)

Side 2: (Covering ears.)
Stop, stop, stop. We don't want to listen. If we don't hear we can't say we know. We don't want to be challenged, to have to make a response. It's not that we don't care, we just want it all to go away. We can't cope. We have enough troubles of our own.

Side 2 uncover their ears. All sit down and keep silence for a few moments.

Leader: Just open your ears and listen to the voices. Listen for justice and truth and hear the voice of God. Open your ears, your eyes, your heart, your hands.

chapter six **seasoning**

**‘You are the salt of the earth;
but if salt has lost its taste,
how can its saltiness be restored?’**

– *Matthew 5.13*

chapter six
seasoning

Without the seasoning of salt, herbs and spices, our food would taste bland and unexciting. Sometimes getting the balance right is difficult and we all have different likes and dislikes, so variety is necessary. We will all probably have experienced times when children – and adults – have declared that they don't like a certain food or flavour without even trying it!

In worship we need variety, too, and a sensitivity to other people's preferred ways of worshipping. Sometimes God can surprise us if we are prepared to 'taste' different things, even if, in the end, we feel more comfortable with something else.

With these thoughts in mind, this chapter is offered as seasoning. It consists, mainly, of smaller items so these can be tried out or slotted into a variety of types of worship to add a bit of extra 'taste'.

Short prayers

Choreographer divine

You danced creation into being
and call us to partner you in the dance.
Teach us the steps of faith
that, whether our life be in quick step or slow,
we may be in tune with the rhythm and flow of your dance.
When we twist and turn in the dark places of our lives
and discouragement and despair trip us,
hold us gently in your arms
and lift us in an arabesque of love and hope.
As we dance to unknown places and new opportunities,
may we encourage others
not just to tap their feet
but also to risk joining in the dance of life.

Creator God

You invite us to share in weaving the cloth of creation,
setting the loom to hold us in the tension of your love,
taking the threads and colours that we offer,
each strand important to your design.

We bring our broken threads of pain and anxiety,
knots of fear, prejudice, sorrow and regret,
the faded colours of broken dreams and promises,
we bring them all for you to fashion
and, in the rhythm of the weaver's shuttle,
through the warp and weft of our humanity,
you weave the bright colours and textures of our love and laughter,
joy and hope, into a beautiful, vibrant cloth of love and justice
to clothe the world.

Liberator God

Long ago you led your people from bondage to freedom.
Forgive us that so often we enslave you,
confine you in creeds and traditions,
imprison you in language and outdated images,
chain you to history and gender,
creating a God who fits our notion of who you are
and where you are to be found.

Liberate us from the shackles of stagnation.
Release us to rise above the barriers of self-imposed limitations.
Open our eyes to see visions of new possibilities.
Unfetter our feet to dance beyond the circumference of our understanding.
Free us to be liberators for those who can only dream of freedom.

God of freedom

Free us from despair
when we feel the weight of the world closing in on us,
when people oppress us with their expectations and demands,
when we feel got at on all sides and don't know which way to turn,
when we feel deserted and betrayed by friends,
when, in false judgement, people wash their hands of us,
when we feel that even you have deserted us,
when we begin to doubt ourselves and your love.
Give us a sense of perspective and a sign of your presence:
a green shoot, springing from a thorn bush,
a glimpse of resurrection.

Longer prayers

Based on John 1.29–42

There are parts for six voices, but they could be doubled up if you have a small congregation. For more effect, Voices 1 and 2 should be heard but not seen. Other voices could be spoken from their places in the congregation or from the front, as you choose.

Voice 1: What are you looking for?

Voice 3: I am searching for a purpose to my life. I am very successful, good at my job, with plenty of disposable income and a nice little nest egg. I have a happy marriage, lovely kids – and yet there is something missing. What is it?

Voice 2: Come and see *(pause).*

Voice 1: What are *you* looking for?

Voice 4: I am searching for justice for my country, freedom from tyranny and war, for basic human rights for our children, food, education, shelter, the right to express an opinion without fear of imprisonment. I am tired of waiting. I don't want to resort to violence, but sometimes it seems that is the only way to get noticed. Where is the answer?

Voice 2: Come and see *(pause).*

Voice 1: What are *you* looking for?

Voice 5: I am looking for an answer to the eternal question 'Why?' Why is there so much suffering and sadness in the world today, so much hatred, anger, greed. Why the Holocaust, why September 11th, why Beslan? Why did my brother commit suicide? Why did my wife, who was a good person and never did anyone any harm, have to die of cancer? Who has the answer? Is there an answer?

Voice 2: Come and see *(pause).*

Voice 1: What are *you* looking for?

Voice 6: I am looking for love and acceptance for my daughter. Her impairment means that she looks strange and, as she is unable to communicate via speech, we are excluded from most social activities. It's not that people are unkind, necessarily – they just don't know how to respond – but we do feel very isolated. It has been a struggle just coping with everyday living. I am so very tired. Where can I find rest and acceptance?

Voice 2: Come and see *(pause).*

Leader: What will we, the Church, show them? Will we show them the *real* Jesus – the man who sought justice, who set the prisoners free, healed the sick, comforted the sorrowful, challenged hypocrisy – or will we show them what so many see – a Church that is divided, talks in a language and hidden metaphors that few understand? A Church that is so often burdened and weary – with maintenance of buildings or its own internal organization – that it struggles to respond when people come seeking a purpose and meaning to their lives, justice and hope, love and acceptance. *(Pause.)*

Voice 1: Come and see …

Voice 2 … and we will show you Jesus.

Prayer of the Beatitudes

Space is left to add relevant names and situations if wished.

Leader: God of the poor in Spirit, we pray for those who are poor, for those who are so desperately poor it consumes their being, so that they are denied the ability to move, think, speak of anything other than their hunger and thirst. We pray for …

(Pause.)

For the poor in Spirit …

All: … the community of heaven will be theirs.

Leader: God of those who mourn, we pray for those who grieve for the loss of loved ones, the children who have lost parents and relatives to AIDS and have no time to mourn or the capacity to grieve before the next carer is taken and they are on their own again, for those who have lost husbands, sons, fathers, mothers, daughters and sisters in the many wars around the world – wars they did not start and many did not want. We pray for …

(Pause.)

For those who mourn …

All: … they will be comforted.

Leader: God of the meek, we pray for those who have no land in which to plant and grow food, for those whose homes and land have been taken away or claimed by others, for those whose land has been tainted by chemicals or devastated by disaster. We pray for …

(Pause.)

For the meek …

All: … they will inherit the earth.

Leader: God of the just, we pray for all who struggle to obtain justice for the underprivileged and the oppressed, who challenge the status quo and work for those who cannot speak for themselves. We pray for …

(Pause.)

For the just …

All: … they will be more than satisfied.

Leader: God of the merciful, we give thanks for the many people who can show mercy and forgiveness, who break the cycle of tit for tat, the eye for an eye and tooth for a tooth theology. We pray for …

(Pause.)

For the merciful …

All: … they will receive mercy.

Leader: God of the pure of heart, we give thanks for the many people who are simply good people, who see the best in all situations, think the best of everyone and who are true to themselves. We pray for …

(Pause.)

For the pure of heart …

All: … they will see God

Leader: God of the peacemakers, we pray for all who work for peace – not just those who work to end war and disharmony but also those who can see both sides of the argument and strive to create peace with justice, often doing so in situations that put them in extreme personal danger. We pray for …

(Pause.)

For the peacemakers …

All: … they will be called children of God.

Leader: God of the persecuted, we pray for all those who are victimized for their beliefs, whatever their faith, for those who languish in gaol or who are denied education or employment, for those who are estranged from family and friends because of the choice they have made to hold fast to their faith. We pray for …

(Pause.)

For the persecuted …

All: … the community of heaven will also be theirs.

Based on Mark 1.9–14

The prayer focus could be a large shallow bowl of water – in a clear glass if possible – set on a table in view of everyone, with blue and white cloths draped from the bowl down to the floor. Have available some white floating candles. The congregation may be invited to light and float candles either between each section, as indicated below, or at the end.

Leader: God of new beginnings, we pray for those who begin their lives today – each one a beloved child of God. We grieve that so many will not live beyond their fifth birthday, that many will spend their lives in hunger, without adequate shelter and with no education.

A candle is lit and laid on the water.

All: May we be baptized with a passion for justice.

Leader: God of new beginnings, we pray for those who want to make a new start today – those trying to break free from an addiction to drugs, drink, gambling – as each one is a beloved child of God. We pray that they may find support, not judgement, help, not condemnation.

A candle is lit and laid on the water.

All: May we be baptized with compassion.

Leader: God of new beginnings, we pray for those who today will make a commitment to another person in a partnership of love, a business partnership or a partnership of support. May they remain faithful and honest in their relationships.

A candle is lit and laid on the water.

All: May we be baptized with integrity.

Leader: God of new beginnings, we pray for those who will move into a new home this week and those who will leave a home they have lived in for many years to go into residential care. We pray, too, for those who have been forced to leave their homes due to war, fear of war, oppressive regimes, drought or famine and are trying to begin a new life in a refugee camp or a land that is strange to them.

A candle is lit and laid on the water.

All: May we be baptized with empathy.

Leader: God of new beginnings, be with us as we continue our journey of faith. As each day dawns with new opportunities, baptize us anew to meet the challenges of this world that we might have a passion for justice, compassion for those in need,

integrity in our relationships and empathy with those who struggle with the challenges of life. Recognizing that each person is a beloved son or daughter of God, baptize us with the restoring water of your love.

All: Amen.

Meditations

The wise men?

You called us wise,
and so we were in many ways,
but not on that day.
It was later we heard
of all those dead children
and the sound of bitter weeping,
forever now to haunt our sleeping.
Rachel crying for her children.
Was it really because of us? Was it our fault?

If only we had kept our eyes on the star.
If only we hadn't made the assumption about where we would find him.

For not keeping our eyes on you,
for not listening for your voice,
for making assumptions about who you are and where you are to be found,
forgive us.

You called us wise,
and so we were in many ways,
but not on that day.
We had seen what we had come for.
We had paid our dues.
Off home another way now, safe from Herod's wrath,
unaware of what anger and fear we had unleashed.
Were we to blame? Was it our fault?

If only we had not been so naive.
Did we really think that would be the end of it,
that Herod would let it be?

When in our eagerness and naivety we do things,
regardless of the consequences,
when we fail to see the hurt, betrayal and debris we sometimes leave behind,
forgive us.

How many Herods down the years have callously killed and plundered with chains of debt, nationalistic fervour, xenophobia and fear of loss of power?

All the Rachels of the world still weep bitterly for lost children.

Is it our fault?
Have we not looked for you in the right places,
not seen you in the eyes of the innocents,
not listened for you in the voices of the poor,
not recognizing or ignoring the Herods of this world?
Have we turned our backs and gone home another way,
unaware of what we've done?

On our journey to worship, give us wonder.
On our journey to honour, give us integrity.
On our journey to serve, give us humility.

Innocents

A voice was heard in Ramah
sobbing and loudly lamenting.
It was Rachel weeping for her children,
refusing to be comforted
because they were no more.

Grab what you can, the soldiers are coming!
In the dead of the night the warning is given,
It's time to leave home, your land, your possessions,
all that you know and all that you cherish,
to flee for your life and the lives of your children.

Mary and Joseph, together with Jesus, travelled as many have travelled throughout history and into the future –
across open fields and fast-flowing rivers,
tramping the hills and dry barren deserts,
hiding in forests, camping by roadsides.

Eyes always searching.
Ears straining
for the marching of feet and the rumble of tanks,
the crack of the guns and the whistle of bullets.
Running and hiding, jumping in ditches,
the modern-day Herods chasing behind.

And so it goes on, in each generation,
old folks and babies, strong men and children,

women with burdens strapped to their backs,
streams of the fleeing, seeking a refuge,
a place to be safe, to live and to die.
Who will give sanctuary? Where is their Egypt?

Through the roof! (Mark 2.1–12)

It seemed a good idea at first, so they persuaded me.
'After all, Jesus has healed others, so why not you?' they said.
They had been good friends to me over the years,
But, when we arrived, a large crowd had gathered.
Crowds are scary enough when you are on your feet,
but lying on my mattress, on a level with knees,
I felt quite anxious.

'It's OK chaps,' I said, 'you've tried your best.
We will never get through to the house,'
But they were not listening.
They had got this far and they were not going to give up.

They were deaf to my cries of 'No, stop now!'
as they mounted the stairs to the roof.
'Don't you worry about a thing,' they said.
'We have a plan. We'll get you to Jesus, somehow!'

Paralysed with fear, as well as illness,
unable to make my feelings known.
'Please take me home,' I cried, helpless and fearful,
but in their task, all-consuming, they forgot about ME.

Have you any idea what it felt like,
being lowered down through the ceiling, with everyone looking?
As I opened my eyes, he was kneeling beside me.
'My son, your friends have great faith,
your sins are forgiven.'

Have you any idea what *that* felt like – my sins forgiven?
Paralysing guilt taken away!
I jumped up, rolled up my mat, off to celebrate with those who had brought me,
ears closed to the mumblings of others who scorned and criticized.

'Who is he to forgive sin?'

I hardly gave a thought to how *he* felt.

The turning of the tables (Mark 11.15)

I'd never seen that side of him before. He was so angry, it scared me. I didn't know what to do. It was so embarrassing. We were just standing in the queue, waiting for our turn. We had saved up what we thought was enough to buy a pair of pigeons – our sacrificial offering for the safe arrival of our son. It's what the Law requires, but we wanted to do it to give Joshua a good start in life.

We must have miscalculated how much we would need, because it wasn't enough. Well, the problem was that the exchange rate was much higher that day than we'd expected. I must say I've never really understood why there's such a difference, but the money-changer said that it was for Temple taxes and you have to believe what you're told, don't you? So, I thought it must be OK.

There were animals everywhere – lots of mess and noise – and the smell, well, it was awful, just like a cattle market. I was pushed and shoved, and we couldn't get near the entrances to the Temple courts. We had to let our place in the queue go so that we could find our friends and see if they could lend us some money. It was then that I noticed Jesus – there in the Temple courtyard with his friends. He was looking at us, and I could see the anger in his eyes. At first I thought it was something we'd done, that we'd broken some law or other, but it wasn't us he was angry with.

Well, he went charging up to the money-changers' tables. 'What do you think you are doing? Stop making my Father's house into a marketplace!' He ran from one table to another, tipping them over. It was as though a great energy had been released in him. Money, pigeons, feathers, stools and tables flew through the air.

From then on, he was a marked man. As far as the authorities were concerned, that was the last straw. His mother told me later how angry he'd been that we were not only being cheated but that our way to worshipping God had been barred by the stalls and the greed of the money-changers.

They crucified him. He was condemned on trumped-up charges of blasphemy. They are still trading in the Temple courts. We never did buy our pigeons, but somehow it doesn't seem important any more.

Invite people to write down on one side of a piece of paper the things that make them angry and, on the other side, the things that made Jesus angry. How do they compare?

Remember the fragrance and the taste

When I was a child, my mother often sent me to the baker's shop to buy a loaf of bread. I always enjoyed this errand because the bread was baked on the premises and came piping hot from the ovens. It was handed over with just a wrap of tissue paper and always had the most mouth-watering of golden crusts.

At each corner of the loaf, the crusts curled and I always broke these off and ate them before I reached home. However, on this particular day, I must have been especially hungry, as four edges did not suffice and, by the time I returned home, the whole of the top of the loaf was pitted with holes where I had picked off the crust.

As I handed the loaf over to my mother, she looked at me suspiciously and said, 'Did the baker sell you this loaf with all these holes in it?' I don't know if my mother was being particularly naive or she was trying to shame me into confession. 'Yes,' I said, without a moment's hesitation and totally unconcerned at telling a lie. 'Well,' she said, 'just take it back to the shop and tell Mr Brown that I want it changed. The mice have obviously been at it.'

I skipped back to the shop and duly repeated the message with no sense of embarrassment or anxiety. Mr Brown looked down at me over his half-glasses: 'No, my dear,' he said, 'you take that loaf back to your mother and tell her that mice don't have teeth that big.' So, the loaf was returned home. I never did admit to having eaten the crust and my relationship with my mother was uncomfortable as I couldn't admit my guilt. My mother didn't trust me to go to the shop again for a long time, but, every time I smell freshly baked bread, my mouth begins to water and I remember.

Short opening acts of worship

In the beginning (John 1.1–5)

Preparation

Display a very large white candle on a single candleholder with a swathe of cloth beneath it – white or white and gold or rainbow colours.

Suitable music would be 'Sunrise' from *Also sprach Zarathustra* by Richard Strauss.

The event

Read the words of the passage from John slowly as the music begins. At the words 'the light shines in the darkness', have someone light the candle. Then, let the music run to the end, afterwards having a moment or two of complete silence. Break it with the words 'God is with us'. Practising this sequence will help with the timing.

Jesus is home (Mark 2.1–12)

Preparation

You will need three people to be the different voices and they can be dotted around the church or room.

The event

Voice 1: Jesus is home.

Voice 2: There's a crowd gathering.

Voice 3: Hurry on down.

All 3 voices: To get a good view.

Voice 1: Jesus is home.

Voice 2: He's getting quite famous.

Voice 3: What will he say?

All 3 voices: What will we do?

Voice 1: Jesus is home.

Voice 2: He's good for a story.

Voice 3: Come, you who are sick.

All 3 voices: Come, all for your healing.

Voice 1: Jesus is home.

Voice 2: Here with us meeting.

Voice 3: Welcome him now.

All 3 voices: With your praise and your prayers.

He's coming!

Preparation

You will need four people to be the different voices. They can be positioned randomly around the church or room.

The event

Voice 1: He's coming.

Voice 2: Who's coming?

Voice 3: Jesus is coming.

Voice 4: Who says?

Voice 1: Paul said.

Voice 2: So when did he say he was coming?

Voice 3: I'm not sure.

Voice 4: Well, today, tomorrow, next week, next year?

Voice 1: He didn't say when, just that he would.

Voice 2: That's no good.

Voice 3: We need to know now.

Voice 4: So we can get the date in our diaries, plan for it.

Voice 1: Perhaps we should start practising now what we are going to say.

Voice 2: Just in case – we don't want to miss him.

Voice 3: I hate it when people come and I'm not prepared.

Voice 4: Will we know when he has arrived? *(Pause.)*

Voice 1: We could imagine that he is already here.

Voice 2: Perhaps he is. *(Pause).*

All 4 voices: (Quietly.)
Wow *(Pause).*

Blessings

These blessings can be used in a variety of ways – individually or several or all, with responses as shown here or read all together by one person, as you wish.

Leader: Blessed are those who do not think that they are all-knowing.
All: For they shall gain knowledge.

Leader: Blessed are those who know when to speak.
All: For they will speak truth.

Leader: Blessed are those who know when not to speak.
All: For they will be honoured with trust.

Leader: Blessed are those who hear both sides of an argument.
All: For they shall have discernment.

Leader: Blessed are those who can stand in another's shoes and not try to tie the laces.
All: For they will have empathy.

Leader: Blessed are those who speak against injustice.
All: For they will be given fortitude and endurance.

Leader: Blessed are those who share their bread with the poor.
All: For their cup will overflow.

Leader: Blessed are those who are open to new ideas.
All: For vision will be theirs.

Leader: Blessed are those who search for God in unexpected places.
All: For they will be surprised by joy.

Leader: Blessed are those who wait on God.
All: For they are the saints.

Leader: God of the poor.
All: Bless us with your compassion.

Leader: God of the bereaved.
All: Bless us with your comfort.

Leader: God of the humble.
All: Bless us with gentleness.

Leader: God of the righteous.
All: Bless us with wisdom.

Leader: God of the merciful.
All: Bless us with forgiveness.

Leader: God of the pure in heart.
All: Bless us with kindness.

Leader: God of the peacemakers.
All: Bless us with understanding.

Leader: God of the persecuted.
All: Bless us with courage.

Dances

Dances of greeting can be used at the beginning of an event, as an icebreaker. Dancers should try to ensure that they maintain good eye contact with one another. Dancing is a non-verbal language, energizing and good fun. Not everyone is able to dance, but watching and encouraging dancers with clapping or smiles is participation in itself.

You are the centre

The music for this dance is 'You are the Centre' from *Fountain of Life* by Margaret Rizza.

Part A

1. Form a circle, assigning people to be alternately 1s and 2s around the circle. All hold hands, placing the right hand downwards (giving blessing) on to the left hand of the person on the right, but the left hand up (receiving blessing) into the right hand of the person to the left.
2. As the music begins, sway slightly from left to right.
3. As the singing starts, break hands and 1s take four steps in, starting with the right foot.
4. …and remain standing still for four beats.
5. Whilst 1s are waiting for four beats, 2s hold hands and walk forward raising arms, then lowering them over the joined arms of 1s (there is now a large linked circle).
6. Turn to the right slightly (still linked) and walk round in the circle to the right for four beats.
7. Turn and take four steps to the left.
8. Turn back to face the centre of the circle.
9. The 2s raise their arms, still linked with the 1s as before, for four beats, then break hands and step back for four beats.
10. The 1s turn to face the outer circle, taking four steps to do so, then take four more steps as they rejoin the 1s to make a full circle.
11. Repeat the above twice more.

Part B

The music changes at this point so you know when to start Part B of the dance. After Part A, the dancers are in a full circle.

1. All hold hands, raise them above the shoulders and move into the centre of the circle for four beats.
2. Hold for four beats.
3. Bringing the hands down slowly, walk back for four steps.
4. Swing from left to right for four more steps.
5. Turn to the right and walk forward for four steps.
6. Turn to the left and walk forward for four steps.
7. Turn to face the centre of the circle.
8. Repeat Part A.

Joyful greeting

The music used for this dance is 'Meryton Townhall' from *Pride and Prejudice* by Dario Marianelli.

1. Form a circle and assign people to be alternately 1s and 2s.
2. The introduction is four beats long, during which the dancers stand ready.
3. Holding hands and facing the centre of the circle, sway from left to right for eight beats.
4. Stepping sideways, all move round in a circle still facing the centre of the circle and all holding hands.

5 All take four steps towards the centre of the circle and four back and repeat.
6 All turn to the right, still holding hands, and walk eight steps to the right.
7 Turn to the left and take eight steps to the left.
8 All 1s turn to the right and all 2s turn to the left – 1s and 2s are now facing each other.
9 Chain for ten, counting 'one and two and …', by giving the right hand to the next person on the right, passing by, giving the left hand to the next person, passing by and so on around the circle.
10 Side step to the left, then back to the right and continue for a total of eight times, counting 'one and two and …'.
11 Chain again for 10.
12 Turn to face the centre of the circle.
13 Take four steps towards the centre and four steps out and repeat.
14 Skip round the circle, moving to the right, until the music finishes.

A Gaelic blessing

This dance was devised at a circuit weekend for the Witney and Faringdon Methodist Circuit.

The music you need for this dance is 'A Gaelic blessing' by John Rutter. As with the previous dances, this is based on a circle. If possible, have in the centre of your group a small member who is light enough to be lifted. That person should adopt a kneeling position during the dance until the lifting occurs.

1 As before, stand in a circle and assign people to be 1s or 2s in turn, but it does not matter if there is an uneven number.
2 As the music begins, all stand still, facing inwards.
3 As you hear the words 'Deep peace of the running wave to you', the 1s raise their arms above their heads and make waving movements with their hands. Meanwhile, the 2s crouch and make waving movements at knee level moving around in time to the music.
4 At the words 'Deep peace of the flowing air to you', the 1s switch to making the crouching movements and the 2s to making the movements above their heads.
5 At the words 'Deep peace of the quiet earth to you', all hold hands and move towards the right and, in time with the music, make a dipping and flowing movement around the circle.
6 At the words 'Deep peace of the shining stars to you', all turn to face the left, lifting their right hands to touch the other right hands in the circle, meeting in the centre like the spokes of a wheel, and move round in time with the music.
7 At the words 'Moon and stars pour their healing light on you', all face inwards, making starburst movements, by clenching the fists, then opening the left then right hands, spreading the fingers upwards towards the sky.
8 At the words 'Deep peace of Christ', all cross arms in 'Auld Lang Syne' fashion to clasp hands with the next person each side, then slowly bend the knees and move forwards slightly to 'sit' the person in the centre on the arms of one or two people. Slowly lift the person so that, at the crescendo, with the words 'of Christ, the light of the world to you', the person in the centre is above everyone, with arms outstretched.

9 At the next phrase, 'Deep peace of Christ to you', lower the central person slowly back down, still with hands clasped, then, keeping hold of each other's hands, bring the arms over them in a blessing-like action.
10 Release each other's hands, then, all turn on the spot, still in a circle, to face out towards the congregation, stretching the arms out forwards in blessing.

The Hora

This is a very simple Jewish dance, on which many others are based. It can be danced to more or less any tune, fast or slow. Try the music 'Hava nagila', which is readily available. Its title means 'Let's rejoice and be merry, arise with joy in our hearts'.

The Hora is performed in a circle and always danced clockwise.

1 Start in a circle, standing with feet together and holding hands.
2 With the left foot, take a step to the left.
3 Cross the right foot behind the left foot.
4 Step to the left with the left foot again.
5 Kick with the right foot, moving it across the left.
6 Step to the right foot with the right foot.
7 Kick with the left foot, moving it across the right.

Just keep repeating this sequence for as long as the music lasts. People can join in and leave the circle at will.

chapter seven **extra portions**

'Love is the poetry of the senses.'

– Honore de Balzac

The following reflection was first used at Durham Cathedral for the Diakonia 19th World Assembly, 20–27 July 2005.

chapter seven
extra portions

Waves of change

Preparation

For a large display, you will need:

- eight lengths of blue or blue/green material (representing a variety of sea colours)
- small circle of blue material
- small length of green or green/brown material
- flattish pebbles
- a few large, rough stones
- large and small seashells
- large deep bowl of water
- large flat dish of water
- smaller bowl of water
- a few flowers or small plants
- three small baskets
- dove templates
- fishing net
- large water jar or jug
- towel
- bread
- grapes
- tear shapes cut from rice paper
- cards containing the Bible passages and questions given for each section below
- recording of sea sounds, such as 'Ocean Surf' from Dan Gibson's *Solitudes: Exploring Nature with Music: The Classics*
- paper and pencils.

For a small display, these elements can be adapted to suit.

On the floor or a table, lay the eight lengths of blue or blue/green material radiating out from the small circle of blue material, placing it in the centre.

On each of the eight pieces of material, place one of the cards containing the Bible passages and questions, as well as the other items suggested for that particular section (see below).

Have the sea sounds playing quietly in the background.

Invite people to move around, spending time at each section reflecting on the questions. They can start at different points and stay for as long or as short a time as they wish at each. Have paper and pencils available for those who wish to make notes.

This could also be used for a led reflection, with people sitting around in a circle while someone – very slowly and with great care – builds up the display, bit by bit, as the passage and questions connected with each section are read, inviting people to participate at each point.

If this is done, a variety of music could be used, such as:

- a version of 'The Lord is my Shepherd'
- Butterworth's *The Banks of Green Willow*
- Bryn Terfel – Simple Gifts recording
- Handel's 'Air' from *Water Music*, Suite No. 1
- Artisan's 'You are there', from the CD *Dancing with Words.*

At the end, people could be invited to share one or two thoughts or the leader could just close with a blessing.

It is important that this is not rushed – give people plenty of time for each part of the exercise.

Contents of each section

Section 1

Bible passage

'I have called you by name, you are mine. When you pass through the waters I will be with you; and through the rivers, they shall not overwhelm you' (Isaiah 43.1).

Display

Pile of flattish pebbles, some bigger rocks and large and small seashells.

Questions

Think of a time when you have felt overwhelmed by something. Who or what helped you in that situation?

Perhaps at this moment you, or someone known to you, are passing through a difficult time. Reflect on these words from Isaiah.

If you wish, take one of the small pebbles and write your name on it, then either take it away with you or put it back in the display and remember – you have been called by name, you are God's own son or daughter.

Section 2

Bible passage

'With joy you will draw water from the wells of salvation' (Isaiah 12.3).

Display

Large deep bowl of water.

Questions

What has given you joy in your life?

Who has saved you from doing something that you would later have regretted, told you the truth and enabled you to look at a situation in a refreshingly new way?

Gently move your hands in the water, allowing it to run through your fingers. Don't wipe your hands dry, but allow them to dry naturally or rub them on your face or arms.

Section 3

Bible passage

'The Lord is my Shepherd. I shall not want. He makes me lie down in green pastures, he leads me beside still waters; he restores my soul' (Psalm 23.1–3).

Display

Place the small length of green or green/brown material at the edge of the blue, together with one or two flowers or small plants.

Questions

Where do you go for rest and relaxation? Where is your green pasture, your still water? Is it in a special place – a lakeside, a river, the sea, a hilltop, a garden?

Think of the last time you were there. When can you go again? Who will you take with you?

Section 4

Bible passage

'Jesus … was baptized … And just as he was coming up out of the water, he saw the heavens torn apart and the Spirit descending like a dove on him' (Mark 1.9–10).

Display

Basket containing dove templates.

Questions

Jesus was baptized at the very beginning of his ministry, the dove descending being symbolic of the approval of God.

Remember for a few moments people who are making new beginnings today:

- those starting a new job
- those moving to a new home
- those beginning a new life in another country.

Every day is a new beginning – what does this mean for you?

Take a dove template and write a name or message on it and either take it away with you or lay it on the blue cloth.

Section 5

Bible passage

'As Jesus walked by the Sea of Galilee, he saw two brothers, Simon, who is called Peter, and Andrew his brother, casting a net into the lake – for they were fishermen. And he said to them, "Follow me and I will make you fish for people" ' (Matthew 4.18–19).

Display

Basket, fishing net and some shells.

If this is being used individually, insert your own name in the space and change the wording appropriately.

Loving God, as we walk along the shoreline of our lives, may we hear your call to us.
... follow me.

When the tide turns in our lives and we are confronted with difficult decisions, may we hear the encouragement of your call.
... follow me.

When following you means letting go of something that is important to us, may we hear the challenge of your call.
... follow me.

When we feel up to our necks and drowning in all the things we have to do and in circumstances that weigh us down, may we hear the comfort of your call.
... follow me.

When we feel off balance, as the sands of pressure and expectation shift beneath our feet, may we hear the strength of your call.
... follow me.

When we feel overwhelmed by waves of powerlessness and inadequacy, and are in danger of giving up, may we hear the power of your call.
... follow me.

Section 6

Bible passage

'A Samaritan woman came to draw water, and Jesus said to her: "Give me a drink" ' (John 4.7).

Display

Large water jar or jug.

Questions
Before anything else was said, Jesus asked the Samaritan woman for a drink. She was surprised at the request, but it was something that it was in her power to do.

We are familiar with asking God for favours, but what might God be asking from us? It will be something that is well within our power to give.

Section 7

Bible passage
'Jesus, knowing that the Father had given all things into his hands, and that he had come from God and was going to God, got up from the table, took off his outer robe, and tied a towel around himself. Then he poured water into a basin and began to wash the disciples' feet and to wipe them with the towel that was tied around him' (John 13.3–5).

Display
Smaller bowl of water, towel, bread and grapes.

Questions
Guests attending a meal in the time of Jesus would have their feet washed on entry to the house. This task would be done, not by the host, but the lowest servant. Jesus, though, performed this task for his guests and they were scandalized.

Do you find it difficult to allow other people to minister to you? Would you rather be the one who is giving than receiving?

Think of a time when someone has tended to your physical needs. How did you feel about it?

Take some bread and grapes and eat silently, remembering.

Section 8

Bible passage
'They will hunger no more, and thirst no more … he will guide them to springs of the water of life, and God will wipe away every tear from their eyes' (Revelation 7.16–17).

Display
Large flat dish of water and a basket containing the tear shapes cut from rice paper.

Questions
Every day, 30,000 children die from hunger or water-related illnesses and 8,000 people die of AIDS. Around 15 million children have lost one or both of their parents to AIDS worldwide.

What is our response to these facts? What action can we take to end suffering caused by poverty, lack of resources and unfair economic and trading systems?

If you wish, float a rice paper tear in the bowl of water as a sign of your commitment to end poverty and help wipe away every tear. The rice paper tears will dissolve eventually.

A blessing

May the God who created order out of chaos be with you in the ebb and flow of life.

May Jesus, who sat and talked with a woman at the well, give you refreshment for your journey.

May the Spirit, who hovers over the waters of life, give you hope and peace.

Journeys in Holy Week

You may wish to play music between the sections below. If so, the following pieces work well:

- parts of *The Trilogy*, Prague Symphony Orchestra, disc 2, Kingsway Music
- selected pieces from Bach's *St Matthew Passion* and *St John Passion* and Handel's *Messiah*.

Sunday: a journey of acclamation

Leader: Jesus rides into the city on a donkey, acting out an ancient prophecy. Crowds welcome him and the city is in uproar. He goes to the Temple late in the day and to Bethany to spend the night with friends.

Read Mark 11.1–10 slowly several times.

Close your eyes and allow yourself to enter the scene in your imagination. Feel the roughness of the donkey's neck and mane, the texture of the cloaks thrown over it.

Sense the nervousness of the young colt as it approaches the unfamiliar smells and sounds of Jerusalem.

Listen to the sounds of the city, the hooves on the street, the noise of people jostling, the shouts of 'Hosanna!'

Watch the faces of those around you in the city. What are their expectations and hopes? What are your feelings at this point?

Imagine Jesus arriving at the Temple. What are the reactions of those around? What do you notice about Jesus as he looks at the whole scene?

'It was now late.' Imagine the return journey to Bethany.

What are the Twelve discussing?

What are you feeling at this point?

Now gently return to the present moment.

Reflect on your own life journey.

Have there been moments of great excitement and acclamation? If so, how did you feel about it? If not, do you see this as a blessing or a regret?

What are the opportunities of moments of public recognition? What are the temptations?

What are the opportunities when you see a friend publicly recognized?

Monday: a journey of anger

Leader: Monday finds Jesus overturning the tables in the Temple. The court of the non-Jews is full of traders and money-changers making a fat profit as they give out Jewish coins for 'pagan' money. Jesus is upset and angry that there are people in this place of worship who are exploiting and cheating others, effectively barring their access to worship. He continues to teach about his kingdom with stories.

Read Mark 11.12–19 slowly several times until you are familiar with the events.

Now close your eyes and allow yourself to enter the scene in your imagination. Be very conscious of the sounds, textures and sights around you. Watch the expressions on people's faces as the events unfold.

As Jesus turns over the tables, notice your own feelings and the feelings of those around you. What are you saying or doing?

Watch the faces of those around you as Jesus is speaking. How do their varied reactions affect you?

What do you think about what Jesus is saying?

'And when evening came, Jesus and his disciples went out of the city.'

As Jesus leaves Jerusalem, come gently back to the present. You may like to reflect on some of the following questions.

- How did you regard the anger of Jesus? Did his anger fill you with enthusiasm for justice or with fear of the consequences?
- How did you react to the possible disapproval of the chief priests?
- How did you feel when 'the crowd was spellbound by his teaching'?
- Think of a time when you have been very angry or experienced the anger of someone else. Did it make you feel uncomfortable or embarrassed? Do you use anger creatively or try to disguise it?

Tuesday: a journey of interrogation

Leader: Jesus answers some tricky questions that people ask him in order to try and catch him out or make him say something that will incriminate him. He skilfully answers questions about paying taxes, his own authority and which of God's laws is the most important.

Read Mark 11.27–12.44 quite quickly.

This is a long passage that contains a fast-moving series of short interviews where different sectors of the community ply Jesus with questions. Imagine what it would feel like to be on the receiving end of such a battery of complicated trick questions. Imagine Jesus seeing the different groups approaching, each with their own agenda and reasons for wanting to trip him up:

- in 11.28, the chief priests, lawyers and elders
- 12.13, Pharisees and men of Herod's party
- 12.18, the Sadducees
- 12.28, one of the lawyers.

Read the text more carefully now and reflect on how Jesus uses his God-given gifts to cope with the situation.

Leader: Imagine the exhaustion of being surrounded by crowds and battered by questions.

Read 12.35–44 and note how, even after these gruelling encounters, Jesus stays to teach and astutely observes all that is happening around him.

Leader: Think of a time when you have been under pressure. How did you stick fast to your beliefs? Were you aware of the motives of others? Were you ready to use your imagination to confront the problem before you?

Remember others who at this moment may be being interrogated or even tortured for their beliefs or political stance.

Wednesday: a journey of hospitality

Leader: Jesus is relaxing in Bethany at the house of Simon. Guests invited to share hospitality would have had their hands, face and feet anointed with olive oil on arrival. Sometimes perfume would be added. As it was so expensive, it was sold in jars with long necks so that the perfume would only drip out drop by drop. Jesus accepts the ministry of a woman and says that wherever the good news is proclaimed in the whole world, what she has done will be told in remembrance of her.

Read Mark 14.1–10.

Imagine that you are one of the guests at the dinner party.

What do you think was being discussed?

The party is interrupted by the woman who gatecrashes. Watch as she breaks the bottle and pours the perfume over Jesus' head. What is your reaction?

Look around and see the reactions on the faces of the other guests.

Look at Jesus' face. Perfume is rolling down his hair and face, on to his clothes and splashing on to the table and the people around him. Imagine the strong scent as the perfume is poured out and see what a mess it makes.

Who comes to clear it up? What happens when the woman leaves? Who else leaves the room?

Have you ever been in a situation where something as startling as this has happened. What was it and what was your reaction?

Thursday: a journey of ministry

Leader: Jesus makes preparation for the Passover meal with his friends – the last supper they will eat together. During the evening, Jesus takes on the role of a servant and proceeds to wash the feet of his disciples.

Read Mark 14.12–25.

Imagine that you are seated at that last supper.

Where are you sitting? Who is next to you? What are you talking about? What is the atmosphere like – solemn, peaceful, thoughtful?

What do you remember about your last eucharistic service? Who were the people sharing that with you?

Have you memories of a meal shared with someone who has since died?

As Jesus moves round to you, imagine his hands caressing your feet, washing them with cool water and patting them dry with a towel. How does it feel to have him kneel at your feet and wash them?

Read Mark 14.26–28.

When they had sung the hymn, they went out to the Mount of Olives.

Listen to some music or sing a suitable hymn, then leave the room.

Life patterns – for personal or group reflection

Take a piece of very thin cotton material – any colour or pattern – that has been cut into a circle the size of a side plate (it could be larger, dinner plate-sized, if wished). Alternatively, coloured thin paper could be used.

Fold the circle in half, then in half again and once more. Take a pair of sharp scissors and cut out shapes that represent the significant encounters or milestones in your life – special friendships, first job, love or loss, your first encounter with God perhaps. Some of these experiences will be good, others may be painful. Make the shapes reflect these feelings, as far as possible, with sharp, pointed shapes as well as round, soft ones. You can cut all round your circle – it doesn't have to be confined to one side – but be careful not to cut all the way across, otherwise your life will fall apart!

When you have finished, put the cut out pieces to one side, as what has been taken out is also an important part of you. Now open out your life.

You will see how beautiful it is. Lay it out on the table in front of you. Like you, it is unique. As you open your life pattern, you will also notice that the shapes you cut out have been multiplied. You may like to look at one or two of the milestones and reflect on the questions below for each of the shapes.

- What sort of experience was it? Gentle or harsh? One that brings you joy or pain?
- Is there anything left to be dealt with?
- Is there anything in the experience that you need to let go of?
- What have you learned from this experience? How has it shaped you?
- Where was God in your experience?

Light a small candle and play some quiet music as you take a further look at your life – 'Morning Glory' from Dan Gibson's *Solitudes: English Country Garden*, Vaughan Williams' 'The Lark Ascending', Mendelssohn's *Songs without Words* all work well, or play something of your own choosing.

Read Psalm 139.

Think of the day or week ahead. What are the things that you will be doing? Is anything going to be difficult or require patience or skill on your part in order to deal with it? Perhaps there are things that you are looking forward to and people you will enjoy being with. Think of these for a few moments, then lay your life pattern beside the Bible passage and hand yourself over to God, knowing that, in God's wisdom and love, all will be well.

Note

If life patterns are used in an act of worship or with a small group, make reference to the fact that, even if some of our experiences are similar, we will each have dealt with them differently.

Invite people to swap their life pattern with their neighbour's. Look at and hold that life in your hands for a few minutes. Encourage people to share one or two of their milestones with each other, but only if they are happy to do so. Otherwise, just reflect on the pattern's beauty and the person who made it, then hand it back to its owner.

Recognize that sometimes we hand our lives over to others or put our lives in the hands of others, but, ultimately, we are responsible for our own responses and need to hold on to our own lives.

A wallhanging can be made by placing, pinning or sewing the life patterns on to a backcloth and making a patchwork of lives to hang somewhere significant for a short while.

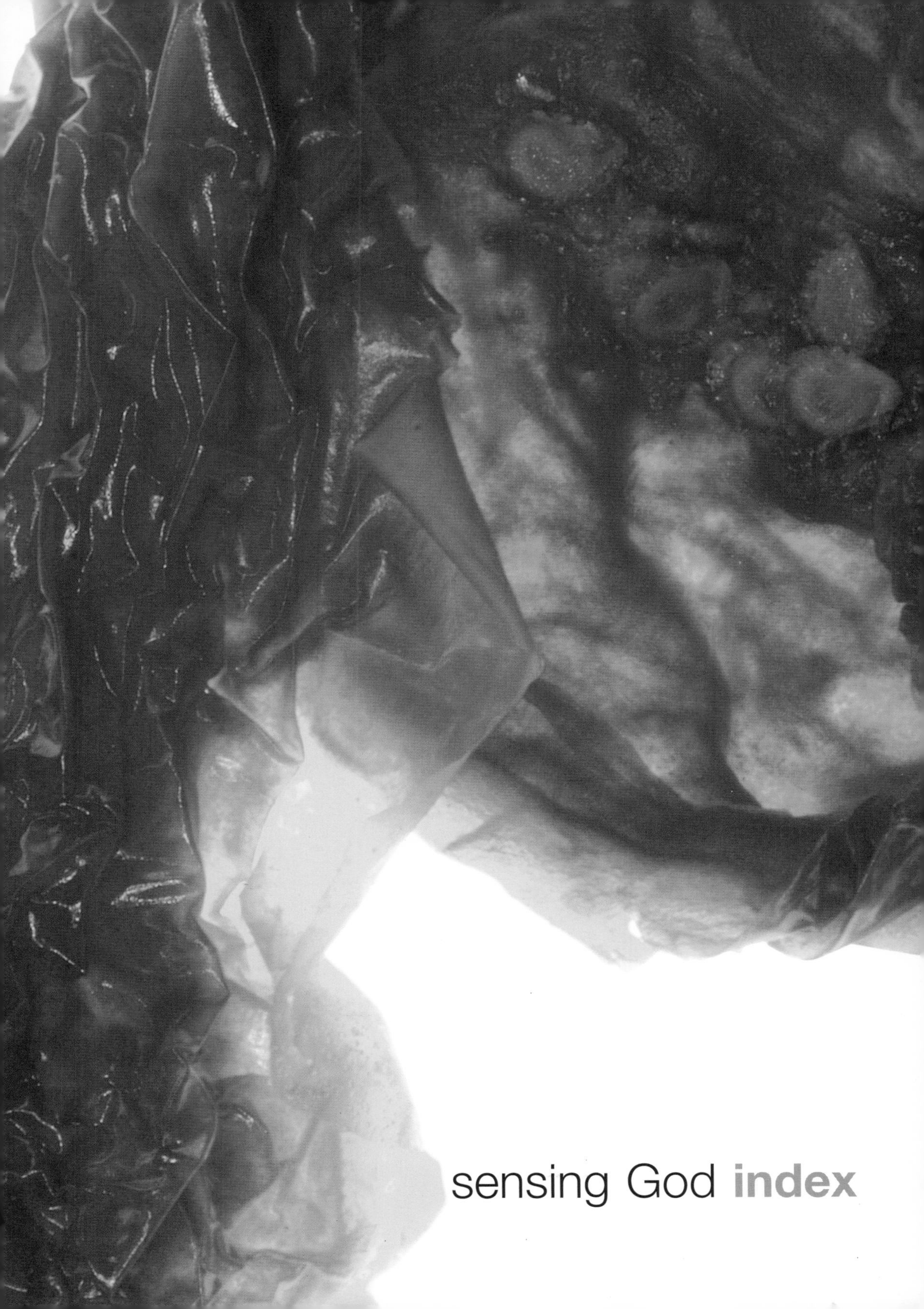

sensing God **index**

sensing God **index**

Title/first line index

Bible references